THE MOST EXPENSIVE GAME IN TOWN

THE MOST EXPENSIVE GAME IN TOWN

*The Rising Cost of Youth Sports
and the Toll on Today's Families*

Mark Hyman

BEACON PRESS
BOSTON

To Evelyn Hyman, with love and thanks
for all those rides to practice.

Beacon Press
25 Beacon Street
Boston, Massachusetts 02108-2892
www.beacon.org

Beacon Press books
are published under the auspices of
the Unitarian Universalist Association of Congregations.

15   14   13   12   8   7   6   5   4   3   2   1

This book is printed on acid-free paper that meets the uncoated paper
ANSI/NISO specifications for permanence as revised in 1992.

Text design by Yvonne Tsang at Wilsted & Taylor Publishing Services

Library of Congress Cataloging-in-Publication Data
Hyman, Mark.
The most expensive game in town : the rising cost of youth sports
and the toll on today's families / Mark Hyman.
p. cm.
ISBN 978-0-8070-0136-3 (hardback)
1. Sports for children—United States. 2. Sports for children—
Economic aspects. 3. Sports for children—Social aspects—
United States. I. Title.
GV709.2H94 2012
796.083—dc23   2011038424

CONTENTS

INTRODUCTION

Greg Centracchio and Brian Bushwell would be the first to tell you that they stumbled—actually, wandered—into their present line of work.

They have been friends since the late 1980s, when they met as students at the University of Hartford in Connecticut. Back then, Centracchio and Bushwell were teammates on the varsity baseball team, a good if not great Hawks squad that won a few more games than it lost. When they graduated, they discussed going into business together. But through the years the college friends never found a project that both could enthusiastically get behind.

Until 2005, when Centracchio got a phone call from his friend. There was a distinct edge in Bushwell's voice, as if he'd hit on something big but wasn't sure how big.

Centracchio remembers his friend posing a question that couldn't have been more unexpected: "Greg, what if we hang a camera on a backstop?" Bushnell had just returned from a trip to a kids' baseball game near his home in New Jersey. For most of the visit, he'd observed parents kibitzing on the edges of the field and taking seats in the bleachers. And he'd thought about the adults who would have loved to be there but couldn't: moms stuck in board meetings, grandparents, aunts, and uncles all living a time zone away.

For those adults, Bushnell suggested, the answer might be a webcam. Nothing elaborate, just an unblinking eye staring down from the chain-link fence behind home plate to record each pitch and swing, and stream the video to a website. Then charge $15 a month for fans of the little players to log in on their laptops. Centracchio, like his business partner a father and a sports nut, remembers what he was thinking as Bushnell explained this simple and yet ingenious plan: Great idea.

It took two years for the entrepreneurs to launch their website, which they named Youth Sports Live, and another two or three for the kinks to be worked out. The partners discovered, among other things, that not all webcams are weatherproof or foul-ball-proof. Nor is it a simple matter to stream multiple youth sports games simultaneously and reliably to the Web.

Now the years of troubleshooting appear to be paying off for Centracchio and Bushnell. Many youth leagues are embracing Youth Sports Live as a boon to parents and a new way to make money. The company contributes a portion of each new subscription fee paid back to the leagues, usually 15 percent. National sports organizations are also getting on board: Little League Baseball, Cal Ripken Baseball, and Dixie Youth Baseball—with millions of telegenic kids circling the bases—all have sponsor deals with Youth Sports Live. In the future, Centracchio and Bushnell plan to expand beyond baseball and softball to kids' soccer, basketball, and a half dozen other sports.

It all sounds so exciting, so cutting-edge—until you speak with Frank Smoll. In 2010, I did. I was writing an article for the *New York Times* about kids' sports and technology, a piece that told the stories of a few pioneering companies, including Youth Sports Live. I wanted perspective on how children are affected by such inventions and was confident that Smoll would deliver. A professor of child psy-

chology at the University of Washington in Seattle, Smoll
and colleague Ronald Smith have written books, developed
coaching protocols, and authored countless scholarly articles
on sports and child development.

Smoll hadn't heard about Youth Sports Live. As I explained the website to him, it was clear that the news I was
bringing was less than welcome to the professor. "It's definitely over the top," he tells me soberly. "I'm sure the people behind this company have good intentions. I imagine
they're thinking, Look, we can have parents and grandparents get close to the situation, really be involved in sports for
these kids. They don't realize they're imposing a system on
children without knowledge of the ramifications. You say it's
a good program for kids, but that doesn't mean it is."

Smoll and I chatted on, with the professor explaining the
surprising (to me) number of ways that a webcam can dam-
age a child's experience in sports: kids feeling under the gun
to perform, judged by an audience of unseen fans, unsettled
by a surveillance camera high above. Only clinical research
would tell the true effect of Youth Sports Live and inventions
like it, Smoll told me. But one outcome might be that some
children would up and quit sports. "It heightens the potential for kids to feel pressured," he concluded. "When the fun
disappears, so do they."

After conducting this interview and others for this book,
I began to think about the subtle if critical difference between improving sports for kids and improving sports for
kids *for adults*. For all its appeal as a business spinning off
revenues for its founders and for youth leagues, is Youth
Sports Live a good idea for children? If not, or even if the
matter is in doubt, should we be embracing it?

There has never been a better time to start a business
selling sports to children and their parents. The reasons are

simple enough: There are more children playing organized sports than ever before—41 million according to the latest estimates. There are more parents and supervising adults invested in the idea that spending on that one extra thing— a travel team, a lacrosse stick, a private lesson—can make a difference in turning their kids into polished athletes. And, of course, there are many more entrepreneurs eager to meet this growing demand.

This book argues that commerce is damaging youth sports. Not all commerce, of course. And, as in the case of Youth Sports Live, not always in ways that are intentional or even evident to those who are selling or buying. Yet commercialization is gnawing away at what is good and valuable about sports for children.

Sports sociologist Jay Coakley, professor emeritus at the University of Colorado, Colorado Springs, and a prolific writer and editor on the subject of kids, adults, and sports, puts it well: "Any time the livelihood of adults depends upon kids doing certain things in sports, there is potential for abuse. Imagine you run a gymnastics gym and have an eleven-year-old who is really good and going to be your marquee star. She comes to you and says her knee hurts. You might be tempted to give her a couple of Advil instead of telling her to sit out for a week," he says.

That's one not-insignificant way that commercialization threatens what is best about kids' sports. Others are these:

Commercialization is damaging the concept of a level playing field in terms of children's access to equipment and coaching. Of course, the field has never been perfectly level, but the era of private coaches, train-with-the-stars summer camps, and the like has only exacerbated the situation. Coakley calls it the privatization of youth sports and believes this phenomenon has been disastrous for children.

Commercialization is obscuring the life lessons of youth sports: striving, succeeding, and failing, always on the merits. In an age when everything seems to be for sale—higher SAT scores, a slot on a college sports team, or your child's name in lights—we've been brainwashed to believe that excellence in sports is a product on a shelf, like laundry soap or a necktie. It isn't, and commercialization is drowning out a vital truth.

Commercialization is the bait that has attracted some very large fish to the pond we call youth sports. For shareholders of Nike, Under Armour, Disney, and other publicly traded companies, the demands for apparel, equipment, and sports drinks add tens of millions of dollars to the bottom line. For kids, that can mean trouble. Gatorade may be the most guzzled beverage on the planet, or it seems so on the sidelines and in the dugouts of youth sports games. Gatorade does all it can to promote its flavored drinks as thirst-quenching and a key to proper hydration. That isn't the whole story. Pediatricians remind us that such drinks fill kids with calories they don't need and can contribute to tooth decay. Or consider Nike. It seems to be committed to turning football into a year-round sport. For good reason: when it becomes one (if it isn't already), Swoosh executives will sell more cleats, cross-trainers, workout gear, and the rest. But is full-time football good for kids? I've never spoken with a pediatrician, neurologist, or orthopedic surgeon who thinks so.

Similarly, the rush is on to turn babies—yes, babies—into athletes. This effort goes beyond irresistible athletic shoes for infants (Nike's Shox Turbo II, a bargain at $41). In this unlikely niche, entrepreneurs pitch baby-exercise DVDs with tips for six-month-olds on soccer, tennis, and golf (adding insult to injury, given that the American Academy of Pediatrics recommends no TV time for children under two).

Media is no less culpable. *USA Today* has created a valuable franchise in its national rankings of high school sports teams, from softball to girls' basketball to football. ESPN has its own proprietary rankings that appear on its slick high school sports website ESPN Rise. To climb these rankings and be a contender for a coveted place in the top ten, it is not enough to win games or even to finish a season undefeated. To reach the top, these schools must be scorched-earth successful. To be noticed means annihilating opponents. Winning margins often reach 50 or 60 points. Sportsmanship be damned.

To say that we are vulnerable to the cacophony of come-ons that surround our kids' sports lives is to understate the situation comically. Really, we're sitting ducks. In other contexts, we're careful shoppers, bringing a coupon-clipper's sensibility to how we buy and from whom. When the subject shifts to sports and our children, that equilibrium is suddenly lost. We have a hard time distinguishing between supporting them and feeding our runaway ambitions for them. The difference isn't apparent until long after the credit card has been swiped.

I've frittered away frightening sums of money on the

baseball education of my sons. The most egregious missteps were inflicted on Ben, the older of the two. Tall and rangy, Ben had a talent for throwing a baseball hard and, unusually for children, where he aimed. As a pitcher, he struck out a lot of Little Leaguers. His weakness was batting. He was not the hitter I decided he should be. Pitches were on top of him before his bat moved from his shoulder. The balls he hit with authority usually rocketed to the foul side of first base. I tried to help (hourly), but that seemed to make matters worse.

I should have left him alone, waiting for the day he would grow into his body. Instead, I seized the opportunity of spring break to enroll him in a hitting school in Jupiter, Florida. The price for three days of instruction under the broiling sun was $1,500. Airfare, hotel, and our dinners at Subway and Chick-Fil-A added an extra $1,000. The attraction was a batting coach I'd heard (from a friend of a friend) worked wonders. We got off the plane from our hometown of Baltimore with Ben's new bat (another $300 investment) and a squeeze tube of sun block. It turned out to be an experience that my son could have lived without. The coach was aloof, and his methods were far too complicated. Ben got nothing out of it.

Michael Messner, a sport sociologist at UCLA and the father of a youth-baseball player, helped me understand that the expensive errors I had made are common among overreaching parents. "There's a thought that your kid has to have every advantage because the world is a competitive place. To give your child that edge is considered a sign of love," Messner tells me. Conversely, parents spending lavishly and perhaps recklessly on youth sports can make the argument to themselves or others that they have not settled for half measures. If there was anything—*anything*—that might have helped turn a kid into a college player or even a big leaguer, it was done. And here are the cancelled checks to prove it.

This book explores both sides of the commercialism equation. It looks deeply at the demand side through dozens of interviews with parents, coaches, and others who either make or observe purchasing decisions. I found public opinion surveys on spending on youth hard to find, so I created my own. At various points in the book, I reveal my inner pollster and share the sometimes surprising results of the business of youth sports poll. I thank all the parents, grandparents, coaches, and other adults who responded, including the rugby coach from Australia.

The second part of the book is an analysis and exploration of the supply side. There aren't any convincing dollar estimates of the youth sports economy, perhaps because it's nearly impossible to define what we mean by it. Spending on a girl's racing swimsuit is in. What about the gas money spent to shuttle a child to an out-of-state swim meet? Or a subscription to ESPN's *Rise* magazine, the glossy publication for high school athletes (the issue in front of me includes the article "Black Leggings: Why They're the Must-Have Training Gear of the Season, Plus Our Six Favorite Pairs"). What about those potent energy drinks in the colorful little cans? The ones that the manufacturers claim aren't marketed to kid athletes (wink, wink) but are a common sight at rec fields and high school gyms?

What is clear is that this amorphous thing we call the youth sports economy is expanding rapidly with no sign of stopping. It's a good time to be selling the stuff that youth athletes have needed (and their parents have been buying) for fifty years—gear, apparel, and shoes, among other categories. It's an equally fine moment to be a Youth Sports

Live, ESPN, or *USA Today*, leveraging technology to reach the wallets of a generation of parents.

Youth sports tourism is making a lot of communities wealthy. Or wealthier. First, they build a sprawling complex of fields and diamonds. Next come the chain hotels and restaurants. Finally, the visitors arrive, in some towns hundreds of thousands of them each year. In Round Rock, Texas, during the height of the girls' softball season, there are so many that traffic backs up for miles, and it's impossible to get a table at one of those new restaurants.

It's all good for the capitalists who surround and sell youth sports. But how is the youth sports economy affecting our kids? And what stresses, financial and otherwise, is it imposing on families? How is the great sloshing of dollars distorting the experience that we want for children when they leap off the starting block or dribble down the lane? Throughout these pages, I'll be exploring those questions and one other: Is there any way to turn off the spigot?

ONE

The Parent Trap

Among the hundreds of people I met during the researching and writing of this book, no one took more interest in
the cost of youth sports than Fran Dicari of Cincinnati. Fran
is an advertising executive, husband, father of three children, and devoted youth sports spectator.

Dicari spends a lot of time supporting his kids' sports
habits, sitting in bleachers and mingling with other parents.
A few years ago, to share his observations and connect with
a wider audience, he started writing a blog called *StatsDad*.
Topics covered vary widely, from hints about taking better
photos at youth sports events to a memorable post analyzing
the sometimes-overlooked question of why girls' volleyball
pants have gotten progressively shorter and tighter over the
years ("I wonder how many girls with potential avoid playing
the game because of the short shorts. If it were one it would
be one too many.").

My favorite department of *StatsDad* is called "Youth
Sports Costs"—exactly what the name suggests. Most sports
parents go through the year spending on their kids' sports
lives—writing a check for tennis lessons or paying cash for
new cleats or pulling out a credit card for expensive racing
swimsuits—without bothering to keep a running total. They
cover the expenses necessary to keep their youth players on

the field, in the same jerseys and cleats as their neighbors' kids, and leave it there. If you asked them what they spend in a year on youth sports, all they could say would be this: too much.

Not Fran Dicari. Not only does he know what's coming out of the family till, so do readers of *StatsDad*. In 2010, Dicari seldom let a receipt for a sports expense pass through his fingers without posting it to "Youth Sports Costs." Before the year ended, Dicari had updated his blog forty-three times. This includes entries for two dozen recycled Pinnacle golf balls ($10) and a pair of UMBRO softball socks ($6). It also was a year in which the Dicari family made expensive sports purchases, and those are listed here, too: two soccer trips to Dayton, Ohio; baseball overnights to Kentucky and Indiana; and then the budget-buster, a journey to the Baseball Hall of Fame in Cooperstown, New York, for which the housing bill alone came to $1,000.

All told, the Dicaris' youth sports bill for 2010 totaled almost $9,000—precisely $8,921. In January 2011, Dicari started counting again. The first entry in his costs list was admission fees to his kids' sports game ($24). Noting his expenses—and posting them in cyberspace—was not intended as a belt-tightening exercise, Dicari tells me. Rather, his point was simply to learn more about his spending. "We were going to support our kids regardless," he says. "The idea came more out of my curiosity. That, and I thought this would generate some pretty good conversation."

There aren't many—or perhaps any—other Fran Dicaris publishing their youth-sports ledgers to the last nickel. Yet money is an ever-more important factor in the sports lives of American families. The effects go well beyond what we feel in our pocketbooks. They can also disrupt what goes on in our heads. From the outside looking in, our decisions can be hard to fathom. In my book on youth sports injuries, *Until It Hurts,* I tell the story of an Atlanta family that poured every available dollar into the golf career of a son, now an accomplished college player. The father explained to me that he and his wife, without hesitation, had stopped buying clothes and going on family vacations. When there was a real money crunch, he'd opted to skip payments on his family's health insurance. "It came down to what we were going to do with that five hundred dollars: pay that or pay for golf," he said.

That's an extreme case but, as I learned speaking with parents and coaches for this book, not that extreme. A veteran coach in a program for highly competitive girls' lacrosse players tells me that, even during the economic meltdown of 2008–2009, sports training was about the last place that parents trimmed their budgets. "I know parents who've lost their jobs. They have no idea when they'll be working again," he says. "Yet they still pull together that $450 to send their kid to a summer camp. Why? Because the college coach [running it] mentioned she had *some* interest in their daughter."

We've come to equate spending on our kids' sports lives with achievement in sports. Conventional wisdom suggests that the more we spend, the more excellent our children become. In a later chapter, I discuss this mindset in the form of the college showcase or combine. Essentially, a high school player, often accompanied by parents, travels to a distant sports complex to audition before a panel of coaches. The more a child can be seen by these coaches the greater the chances of impressing one. Or so the thinking goes. Some families attend a dozen or more such events.

"In our society, there are parents who believe they can pay for the success of their child," says Roc Murray, the baseball coach at Rocklin High School for nearly twenty years and the California Coaches Association's coach of the year in his sport in 2010. "I'm not against camps or private coaches. I'm against superficial decision making [by parents]. I'm against the mentality of keeping up with the Joneses, which is where we are in the United States," he tells me. "It's not a good place for kids to be. I am a coach and teacher. I don't believe any kids' success lies with me. Success lies within them."

This chapter takes a closer look at the price of play through the experiences of three families living thousands of miles apart in Ohio, Kansas, and California. Their children are different ages and play different sports. They have different hopes and ambitions for their children in sports. They've never met.

Fran Dicari grew up on the East Coast and moved to Ohio almost twenty years ago. He's married to an exceptional photographer, whose action shots are featured prominently on his blog, *StatsDad*. The oldest of the Dicaris' three children is a college student. They also have a son, thirteen, and a daughter, ten.

Next are the Andersons of Lawrence, Kansas. Dennis Anderson is the managing editor of the *Lawrence Journal World*, a fine newspaper in which coverage of the hometown team, the University of Kansas Jayhawks, is unparalleled. Anderson and his wife, Julie, have two sons, Eric, a college student and Thomas, fourteen, who is in high school. Thomas loves hockey, and, as I learned from Anderson, if you live in Kansas and your child loves hockey, your life is not entirely normal.

Finally, there are Cheri and John McKinney of Santa Barbara, California. McKinney is a freelance writer and a former contributor to *Runners World*. Her husband, John, aka the Trail Master, was the hiking columnist for the *Los Angeles Times* for seventeen years. He is a great advocate of all forms of exercise, especially those that involve a walking stick. The McKinneys' have a teenaged son, Daniel, who is an impressive baseball player in Santa Barbara and on the road, which, during recent summers, has included team trips to Steamboat Springs, Colorado, and Cooperstown, New York.

I met these families through a mutual friend named Survey Monkey, a statement that will require some explaining. About six months into this book project, I decided that, though I'd spent considerable time conferring with coaches, entrepreneurs, historians, archivists, sociologists, and engineers, I needed to speak with more parents. Not just any parents but those covering a wide demographic, parents who could address all manner of questions I had about kids, money, and sports

I spent a few hours shaping my ideas into ten pithy questions about the business of youth sports and, with the help of the virtual pollster Survey Monkey, created an online survey. Next, I approached the Positive Coaching Alliance, a national nonprofit that promotes sportsmanship and responsible sports parenting, asking if it would link to the poll in a weekly e-mail blast that goes out to thousands of PCA followers. PCA director Jim Thompson agreed to send it out.

I had little idea what the response might be, but I was hopeful I might get twenty or thirty shout-outs. Fifty, I thought, would be a deluge.

On a Thursday afternoon, the PCA e-mail launched into cyberspace containing this embarrassing if entirely accurate headline: "Help Mark Hyman Write His Next Book!" Three minutes later, the first form pinged my in-box (it was a simple survey to fill out). In five minutes, I'd received twelve. After an hour, there were fifty. A week later, about two hundred parents and coaches had accepted my offer to report back from the pool decks, gymnasiums, and check-out lines of Youth Sports, USA.

The survey takers wrote from all parts of the country and the world. They shared tales of girls' club hockey in Vermont and flag football in South Florida. Their comments suggested that the escalating cost and commercialization of youth sports was giving a lot of parents heartburn. These replies, among many others, stick with me:

> "I'm a single mom and having kids in travel soccer is very expensive (well, whether you're a single parent or not—it's expensive). Now teams have parents on monthly payment plans (like a car payment!). Maybe someday this great country of ours will figure out a way to develop youth sports without all the expense."

> "For profit club sports are the biggest rip off."

> "Parents will stop at no cost to pay for the best coaching or equipment for their kids. I have seen thousands of dollars spent on nonsense items and camps because of names and name brands, without any considerations for what they may be getting in return."

> "It's sad to me that youth sports are really not all about true talent anymore. With the new technology and travel and showcase teams being where all the scouts go it's turned into a rich person's game. If you don't have the money, you are a lot of steps behind."

> "The 16 families on the team spend a combined $80,000 for the season. Crazy, I know."

I'd hoped feedback would trickle in. Instead I got a tsunami. The parents and coaches who wrote back were frustrated, resigned, exasperated, bemused; others struck me as just plain angry. Yet most parents seemed committed to keeping their kids in the game no matter the cost.

The McKinneys of Santa Barbara; the Andersons of Lawrence, Kansas; and the Dicaris of Cincinnati were among those who replied. Their comments on the survey and in follow-up interviews merited inclusion on these pages, and I thank them.

Many of the parents I spoke with explained that sports were not merely a physical outlet for their children, that the benefits went beyond burning off energy. That was the case for the McKinneys and their son, Daniel. Early in our conversation, Cheri McKinney explained that her son is dyslexic. His diagnosis in the second grade came as a relief to the family, for it explained much about Daniel's indifference to school and his struggles to keep pace with classmates. "School is a real chore. It's not where he excels," McKinney explains.

Things improved for Daniel after the dyslexia diagnosis. His parents moved him to a new school with less structure—and they began to understand that their child thrived on physical activity in ways that others kids his age did not. "One of the symptoms is not only the reading [difficulty] but needing to be outside a lot," McKinney tells me. "When he's active in baseball, he can really hyperfocus. He tells me he can see the seams on the ball as it's being pitched. It makes him a terrific hitter."

McKinney pauses for a moment and adds, "Baseball is a place for him to be very successful."

With so much for their son to gain from sports, it's no wonder that John and Cheri McKinney have supported him wholeheartedly. In Santa Barbara, where baseball weather prevails year-round, there have been years when Daniel played all but two or three months. He has also worked with a private coach, Orlando Guerra, who Cheri McKinney refers to as a mentor and friend as much as an instructor. McKinney sees this investment in time and money for her son as prudent. Given the chance to spend again on team registration and the private lessons, she tells me she would. No hesitation.

What we end up talking about longest—and what McKinney is most animated about—is something relatively new to her experience as a sports parent, overnight trips. In the past two years, as her son has improved as a player and stepped up to more competitive "travel" teams, he and his parents have been baptized into the world of long-distance baseball trips. Long-distance, expensive baseball trips.

McKinney and her husband have chaperoned their son on trips to Steamboat Springs, Colorado, and Cooperstown, New York. They agreed to the trips in part because their son was a member of a travel team and because, with minimal input from parents, the coaches announced that the team was going.

There's always the option—a theoretical one at least—to say no or hold firm to the position that sending children thousands of miles from home for games that could be played in their communities is excessive. But, as with most things, challenging the status quo in kids' sports entails risk. A coach might be put out, and there could be repercussions. The bad feelings ultimately might hurt a child, who could lose favor with a coach and perhaps playing time. For a parent uncertain about a coach's methods, it's something to think about.

The McKinneys' travel team booked a tournament in Steamboat Springs. Months before the planned departure, parents met with the coaches to discuss what would be involved. Cheri McKinney remembers a sense of anxiety settling over the discussion as they read off the list of required purchases: team pins, matching equipment bags, and so on. Cheri recalls a morale-building speech in which one told the parents that the children on the team had "earned the right" to go on their Colorado trip and that the parents "can't take that away from them."

McKinney remembers thinking about her thirteen-year-old child and his teammates and asking herself, "Really? I don't think they have a clue."

The trip cost the McKinneys $1,500. That was only because Cheri McKinney and son Daniel did it on the cheap. They drove from Santa Barbara with another family to the game site, a trip of more than a thousand miles in each direction. Driving time was more than seventeen hours. In Colorado, mother and son shared a condo with another family. They cooked their meals rather than eat out.

McKinney would have gotten equal value for her money if she'd loaded up on Enron stock. The team lost more than it won. Her son barely played. When he played poorly, the coach yelled at him. Neither mother nor son enjoyed being far from home. "My kid loves familiarity. The more changes in his regular routine, the worse he does," McKinney says.

I ask McKinney what her son got out the trip.

"I don't think he benefited from Steamboat at all."

The McKinneys also sent their son for a supposedly dreamy week at Dreams Park in Cooperstown. Cheri McKinney came away with the same general feeling that a dollar spent sending a child cross-country to play baseball is pretty much a dollar wasted.

"The problem is, there is no roadmap for parents," McKinney says. "When we spend on a reading tutor, we know how to measure that . . . reading is a necessary skill for the future. How do you measure the value of this? There's a level of flattery when someone tells you your kid is good, that if your kid works hard he may be really good. When you hear that, why wouldn't you do everything for your child? There's a guilt thing if you're not taking advantage of every 'opportunity,'" she says.

Dennis Anderson of Lawrence, Kansas, is so committed to helping his teenaged son, Thomas, keep playing hockey that once a year he finds himself sitting at a card table at a local country club playing multiple hands of Texas Hold 'Em poker. Some of his fellow players he's never laid eyes on before. Others he knows well—they're the moms and dads he spends months at a time hanging out with at the ice rink during the long season. Hockey is the most expensive sport for children, if you're not counting equestrian and big-game hunting. The tab to keep one child on skates and on an organized team easily can run to $5,000, and Anderson estimates that each year his son remains in the sport costs the family $8,000; that's more than college tuition for his older son. "Other than housing, it's one of our top expenses," Anderson says.

It would be even higher if not for the resourcefulness of hockey parents in Kansas, who offset team expenses with a golf tournament and, Anderson admits sheepishly, those Texas Hold 'Em poker nights, attended by a professional card dealer and forty to fifty friends, and intended as fundraisers for the team. Some don't know the children whose sports lives they are underwriting.

Anderson and I traded several e-mails about the economics of youth hockey in which I could almost see him scratching his head about adults playing poker to pay for youth hockey. Later, when we spoke by phone, he told me, "This all eventually comes around. There will be a friend selling raffle tickets for his son's basketball team. It doesn't end with your family. It's a vicious circle."

Why do the Andersons put themselves through it? Dennis tells me about those moments when he is sitting in a chilly rink watching his son play defense and the horn blows signaling the end of the game and Thomas skates toward his teammates on the bench.

"I do it for the look on my son's face," Anderson says. "It sounds like a cliché, but it's not. He's a good kid. He works hard at school, gets straight As. Ever since he was a little kid, it's always been fun watching him skate and have fun. As a parent you want to see your son do well, and this is something he does consistently well."

We spoke about the logistical challenges attendant to living to Kansas and raising a child who yearns to see the puck dropped at center ice. Anderson explained that there were no organized teams for Thomas in Lawrence. This season he was playing for a travel team based in Kansas City, forty miles away.

He went on to explain the practice and game schedule, which, in a word, is daunting. Twice a week, Dennis Anderson and his wife, Julie, must get Thomas to his practice in Kansas City, forty-five minutes in the car each way. On top of that are the games, forty-five to fifty each season. The home games required the standard forty-five-minute commute. The road games are in St. Louis, Omaha, Des Moines, and other mostly distant places throughout the Midwest, including, over Presidents' Day weekend, an especially wearying drive to Chicago or Denver. "That's eight or nine hours," Anderson tells me.

The Andersons drive their 2004 Honda Pilot with 140,000 miles, or, on longer trips, the family's 2000 Dodge Minivan with an odometer reading of a mere 120,000. They stay in cramped hotel rooms, often four to a suite, doubling up with other fathers and sons. As the expenses pile up, there's an additional irritant of feeling taken advantage of by the for-profit companies that often run youth sports tournaments. Anderson has been to dozens of these weekend hockey tournaments, enough to suspect that money is being pulled from his pocket in ways that often are not disclosed to parents. The tournament promoters, he tells me, "run everything from T-shirt sales to booking hotels." In one upcoming tournament, he tells me, "each team must stay in a tournament hotel. That's part of the deal. The tournament organization [and] the local youth organization get cuts from the hotel. It's common knowledge among parents that this is happening, and there is always grumbling about it over the quality, price."

The prevailing attitude, though, is that there's little point picking these financial nits. Commercialization has become far too entrenched. It's hopeless to fight Best Western. Or Pizza Hut. Or, above all, Nike.

"When I think about how much we've spent over the years, I'd say we're nuts," Anderson tells me. "I've had the conversation with parents many times, and they think they're nuts too.

"Everything you see at these tournaments, from a piece of clothing to photos of your kid, there's somebody behind it making a profit. How many e-mails have I gotten saying, 'Open this,' 'Take a look at your kid,' 'Buy this photo.' The discouraging part is that all we want to do is watch our kids play. Why do we have to put a dime or dollar in somebody else's pocket?"

After conducting interviews with dozens of parents like him, it's my view that Dennis Anderson speaks for many, perhaps most, moms and dads of youth athletes. Something is amiss, we realize. The sports life of adolescents should not be a four-figure annual investment. Yet when faced with a choice to spend or not to, we seldom choose the latter. The result can reflect a glaring weakness in judgment. One of the most startling examples is the strange tale of Jason Anderson (no relation to Dennis Anderson). Anderson is a youth coach and a flim-flam man. His nefarious scheme cost a handful of parents in Rapid City, South Dakota, more than $30,000. He's serving ten years in prison after pleading guilty to grand theft by embezzlement in 2011.

Jason Anderson was Harold Hill, the blustery band leader in *The Music Man*. Only Anderson's victims thought they were buying a spot on an all-star kids' baseball team. Anderson came to Rapid City and wheedled his way into the confidence of the owner of a local batting cage and then of a half-dozen parents. Apparently, it wasn't hard. Anderson announced plans to form a traveling youth team for the best players in the area, called Team South Dakota. Then he began hitting up parents for hefty registration fees. If they offered any resistance, Anderson told them that their children were stars, that they couldn't afford to miss an opportunity like this, that their children were, on average, nine years old was beside the point. "He told me that my son was a great ball player and that he wanted him on his team," one of the parents, Ken Packwood, told the website Inside Dakota Sports.

Packwood paid Anderson $6,300—in cash. Other parents advanced him thousands of dollars more. Then they waited for Anderson to deliver on his promises of flashy uniforms and a road trip to Cocoa Beach, Florida. After weeks of waiting, there were no uniforms, no Cocoa Beach, and no Jason Anderson. He could not be found. Lawsuits and criminal charges followed.

At Anderson's sentencing, almost a year after he'd run off with the money, another parent told the judge that his son showed much potential as a baseball player before the incident. Now the child refused to play the game. Anderson spoke too, admitting that he'd used the money on drugs and gambling. Then he told the parents and children in the courtroom that he was "sorry for ruining your dreams."

We will pay lavishly to help our children pursue their sports dreams. A number of years ago, I wrote an article for *BusinessWeek* about the IMG Academies in Bradenton, Florida. It's a remarkable place: 180 acres of sports fields, high-tech fitness centers, and other training facilities set amid Bermuda grass and swaying palms. The academy began as an elite sleepover school for kids with exceptional athletic ability and drive. Andre Agassi, Carling Bassett, and Maria Sharapova spent time in a tennis boarding school based here. So have many prominent golfers. Their lives are busy and highly structured. In the morning, they attend classes at the Pendleton School, where the kid athletes sign up for traditional academic courses. Afternoons and weekends are devoted to sports training.

Over the years, IMG has learned two things. First, maintaining a posh sports campus on tuition collected from a few elite athletes is a major challenge. Second, there is money in marketing elite sports training to ordinary youth athletes.

With that in mind, IMG began opening its doors to all with the ability to pay. I spoke with one such girl, a very eager tennis player, who was thrilled to be in school there despite having not an ounce of Steffi Graf in her. Her goals were to trim her figure and improve her tennis as much as possible. "I hadn't really played ever. I used to take a lesson once a week about two years ago," she told me then. She was thrilled with her progress. "I came here and my game skyrocketed. I must be 100 times better than before."

Arrangements like these come at a price. In 2011, room,

board, tuition, and sports tutoring for a young golfer at the IMG Academies ran $54,735 per year.

Sound pricey? Then consider the students of Steve Clarkson, a former college football player at San Jose State and these days a quarterbacks' coach. But not any coach. Clarkson may be the best quarterback teacher anywhere— certainly the most expensive. Clarkson charges $700 an hour. His students include sons of former National Football League great, quarterback Joe Montana; National Hockey League Hall of Famer Wayne Gretzky; and rapper Snoop Dogg. More than two hundred of Clarkson's pupils have gone on to play major college football. Several are playing in the NFL. Not all who come to Clarkson are ready for prime time, though. One recent student, a fifth grader, weighed ninety-six pounds. Presumably, his parents believed in their son's potential and, as important, had the deep pockets to pay for Clarkson's schooling.

This is not the way most of us live or spend. For a surprising number of parents, just keeping their kids in sports requires financial sacrifice. One parent I spoke to who asked not to be named explained that her child had played five different sports. That was during good times for the family. When the economic downturn hit, a lot changed. "We have cut back to three sports, and we have one sponsor [a family friend] that paid for his football and soccer fees," the parent says.

Luis Pico of Plantation, Florida, has two daughters who love volleyball. The fees for teams, tournament, and such are prohibitive. So, he says, "I have a sideline as a coach." Pico coaches high school and private club teams, and serves as a coach at clinics and summer camps. The money he earns as a volleyball coach and helper offsets the expense of the total-immersion volleyball experience that his children are getting. As a coach with these various programs, Pico qualifies for the in-house discount. That drives the price down further. Without this benefit, Pico would be looking at a per child annual volleyball bill of about $9,000. He writes telling me that would not be a possibility for him.

He is pleased that he can give his children this experience. But there are regrets, too. In an ideal world, Pico tells me, his girls would not be full-time volleyball players. But he feels hemmed in by financial constraints and realities. "I can't afford letting them have the experience to try any other sport because I don't have the resources to pay full tuition," he says.

Few parents grasp the financial realities of youth sports as clearly as Fran Dicari. When we spoke in November, he was looking back on his son's select baseball season, a schedule of about seventy games. His daughter had just been chosen for the local Amateur Athletic Union basketball squad, which he described as one of the top in the region. "We're going to Louisville tonight," he told me. When I scanned Dicari's blog in January, I learned that his son was also playing middle-school basketball on the school's top team. Dicari clearly was pleased and proud but also sober about his son's talent in the sport: "As I have frankly stated before, my son made his school's top basketball team because of heart and hustle and not for his skills. I write this openly because my son is self-aware. My son understands that basketball is a sport he will most likely not play competitively beyond 8th grade. He plays for fun. Regardless, like any other experience, this may help define who he is going to be."

For Dicari, the motivation is to do all that he can to help his children become proficient enough in baseball, basketball, or another sport of their choosing to become high school varsity athletes.

"College is hugely competitive. I don't even think about college sports for my children. Pro sports are even less realistic. To experience high school sports is kind of what drives us," Dicari tells me. "Some of the fondest memories of my life are about playing high school sports. We want to put our kids in a position to play. And that will not be easy for them, because the high schools they will be going to are the most competitive in sports in the country." This is not hyperbole. Dicari told me his son likely would be heading off the next year to Cincinnati's Archbishop Moeller High School, an athletic powerhouse in many sports and with particular star power in baseball. Moeller graduates include nearly a dozen players who have played in Major League Baseball and one, Ken Griffey Jr., all but guaranteed a place in the Hall of Fame. The season starts early at Moeller. In January 2011, with the first games months away and snow piled high— there were exactly four days without some sort of workout planned.

Dicari's teenaged son works almost as hard playing for the Cincinnati Stix, an elite travel team. While this super-competitive brand of ball supposedly prepares kids for a future at schools like Moeller, Dicari observes that it "brings out the worst in parents. Those who spend a lot of money think they're owed something—more playing time, better calls from the refs. It's definitely more intense than recreational sports."

In some ways, Dicari considers himself an exception. "There are times when I feel like my son has been wronged in certain things. I hardly ever say anything. There are times you sit on the sidelines and bite your lip," he says. "But I've been a coach before. I know how difficult it is to manage twelve kids and the adults. All parents see their kids as better than they really are."

The emotional and financial investment that the Dica-ris and families like them willingly make was evident when Fran happened to describe the uniforms of the Stix. There is no single uniform. Rather, the young players mix and match from a remarkable array of options. All told—two color pants (gray and white), two color jerseys (grey and white), and team undershirts in three colors (in perspiration-wicking fabric, not cotton). The Stix have three team colors: gold, blue, and cardinal red. Players purchase a cap in each color. There are different color cleats and stirrups (socks). Warm-up jackets come in a color rainbow too.

Not surprisingly, *StatsDad* had calculated the total of uniform combinations. His calculator told him it was seventy-two.

"We thought the coach was nuts," Dicari says of this re-markable selection. "The kids loved it."

That sums up the challenge for sports parents, doesn't it? Our kids always prefer more. Sporting goods companies are forever tempting us with more. Same with the sports drink companies and even the private tutor at the local gym.

It begs the question for young athletes: Is more always better?

TWO
Baby Goes Pro

Doreen Bolhuis is a trim, energetic woman who speaks quickly and with absolute conviction. Listen to her for ten minutes and you come away thinking, "Maybe she's right." Even when the medical evidence suggests she isn't.

Bolhuis lives in Grand Rapids, Michigan, where for many years she has operated a gym for young children, teaching them to jump, dance, and move athletically—a set of skills she refers to as "physical literacy." A few years back, Bolhuis's entrepreneurial side asserted itself again when she launched Gymtrix, a pioneering company that promotes sports exercise for babies and toddlers.

Correct: sports for babies.

From a website with lots of testimonials and plenty of video, Gymtrix markets sports DVDs for babies as new to the world as six months old. To me, that seemed absurdly young to be introduced to sports (or to anything more ambitious than a brightly colored mobile circling a crib). But to Doreen Bolhuis, waiting until a baby is six months old to get her going in sports can feel like parental foot-dragging. "With the babies in our family," she tells me, "I start working them out in the hospital."

If you're having trouble picturing a baby sports workout, surf over to the Gymtrix website, where you can watch excerpts from several Gymtrix videos. I've listed some here, with the official descriptions (my comments follow in parentheses).

"Batter Up: Teach your baby to swing and hit—it does much more than improve their future batting average. These activities increase baby's eye-hand coordination and jumpstart brain development."

(It looked like batting practice for babies. Kids grip a paper-towel holder and swipe at a balloon.)

"Jammy Jump: Babies laugh and giggle their way through our Running Man, Ride the Horsy, and other games. Best of all, they strengthen their large muscle groups with every fun movement."

(Moms hold on with two hands as babies leap from chairs and sofas to the floor and back. Moms seem to be having more fun than the babies.)

"Kick It: As babies learn to walk and run, they need to control their legs and feet. You and baby will love these simple games that enhance brain development."

(Evidence, if any is needed, that infants do not know how to kick.)

Bolhuis impressed me as a true believer in the notion that babies have untapped talent that is frittered away. "That is really where I hope to make an impact, helping parents and educators become aware how much babies can do," she tells me. "We sell them short because they can't speak yet. But babies are all about learning how their bodies work and learning about movement patterns. When we guide them, they can learn much more quickly than if we leave it to chance and hope they'll figure it out.

"Think of it this way: We read to babies. We put them on our laps. We show them picture books. We start them on the path to academic education. The exact same thing happens with physical literacy. When we take those tiny bodies and we show them movement patterns, they develop positive emotional associations with movement. They enjoy moving their bodies and feel good about that."

Bolhuis told me of children who have gone through her program and on to great things in sports. In her own family, she'd seen remarkable outcomes—babies and toddlers who were outperforming their peers because they'd been taken by the hand and taught how to use their bodies, not dumped in cribs or car seats and expected to figure out the path to coordination by themselves. Of these advantaged children, Bolhuis says, "At three months, they're usually a month ahead of their peers in physical development. At six months, they're usually about three or four months ahead. At a year, they are almost a year ahead. Their pediatricians are always blown away by how coordinated, how strong they are. Every child is capable of that. It should be what we expect of our babies, but we don't. We let them lay around. We containerize them. We hope they will figure out how to move."

As Bolhuis and I spoke, neither of us knew that she would soon be at the center of a national debate—granted, a brief, peripheral one—about sports training for babies and toddlers. Within a few months of our conversation she was explaining—and defending—her views on CNN and *Today*, views that became the impetus for a Katie Couric commentary closing the *CBS Evening News*.

I confess to being partly responsible. In 2010, I wrote a piece about Bolhuis and other baby-sports pioneers for the *New York Times*. At that point, I'd written about a dozen articles on kids and sports for the *Times*. But this one clearly was provocative and perhaps even odd. It tapped into a wide vein of angst and insecurity among parents about when to start a child in sports. The fear of waiting too long nudges us to search out soccer leagues with nursery-school divisions for three-year-olds. Yet there must be an age that we can all agree is just too young. There must be.

The editors at the *Times* apparently thought it was a worthwhile parenting or sports-business story. To my surprise, the article ran on the front page under the headline, "For the Goal-Oriented Parent, a Jump Start in Sports."

For a week, the article ranked among the most e-mailed *Times* articles. The day after publication, it triggered more than one hundred reader comments on the *Times's* website. They ranged from "What's the big deal?" to "You're joking, right?" to admonitions not to be taken in by the commercialization of childhood. Wrote one reader: "Why leave childhood to children? How about microchip implants for children? Leaving nature alone seems wimpy these days." Another commented, "Parents, when anyone asks for your money because they want to teach your toddler, say NO! Toddlers don't need to be taught; teaching them only gets in their way. Infants and toddlers need to be encouraged to pursue the activities they intrinsically desire to do. The only way to know what a toddler needs to work on is to leave him alone."

These readers weren't reacting to Gymtrix only. Other companies operating in the unusual niche of sports experiences for babies and toddlers also were mentioned. These included Lil' Kickers, a national soccer program for kids starting at age eighteen months (a photo accompanying the *Times* article showed a nineteen-month-old boy decked out in a Lil' Kickers shirt and pants, teetering on his Velcro-strap sneakers, poised to kick a soccer ball through a hula hoop. Or fall on his tush.). And there was Baby Goes Pro, a Florida-based company producing sports DVDs for children starting at nine months. The company name generated lots of reaction. A friend who'd read the article sent me a brief e-mail on that point: "'Baby Goes Pro'?? Initially I thought I was reading *The Onion*."

I'm convinced of the sincerity of the businesspeople behind these ventures. This chapter isn't meant as a challenge to their motives or integrity. It is a study in the psychology of the youth sports marketplace The products on the shelves at the local sporting goods store stretch for city blocks, and services to aid kids in the finer points of serving, swinging, and tumbling have never been more available. But strip away the packaging and the promises, and what ultimately is being sold to parents is hope. Hope that money really does buy sports excellence.

Baby Goes Pro? It's a clever branding strategy. And it hits us where we live, in the land of dreams and aspirations. Is the DVD worth twelve bucks? That's not even the question. Is the dream worth twelve bucks?

The impulse to polish our children even before they can walk or talk is neither new nor limited to sports. It's been in the cultural ether for a century, and its most effective promoters, typically are folks with something to sell—a book, a DVD, sometimes a state of mind.

A history of this movement is laid out in an illuminating book, *Buy, Buy Baby*. Author Susan Gregory Thomas traces the roots of the professionalization of child-rearing to the late eighteenth century, when, she notes, women "were for the first time in history exhorted to take on the role of motherhood not just as an avocation but as a vocation."

She recounts how in the 1940s toy company advertising campaigns began to connect children's play with children's emotional development. The period also marks the time when toymakers began hiring psychologists to endorse their latest batch of playthings for babies and toddlers. Gregory Thomas describes a Playskool ad in a 1946 issue of *Parents Magazine* that shows a baby about to drop the top ring onto a stacker toy and ad copy that suggests this was fine example of learning by doing: "Playskool educational toys are designed in co-operation with child psychologists," the ad read. "They direct the play instincts into channels that build muscular control, eye-hand coordination, color and shape perception."

Whether Playskool sold millions more stacking rings by invoking buzz phrases like "muscular control" and "eye-hand coordination" is anyone's guess. Certainly, efforts to sell merchandise around early-childhood development increased in the decades that followed.

As Gregory Thomas tells it, one of the oddest sales pitches concerns a company named "Prenatal University." The Hayward, California, company was founded in 1979 by an obstetrician-gynecologist who created a class for expectant mothers that taught them "how to channel a fetus's attention, help her build a useful vocabulary, and learn lullabies." This made Gymtrix's "Batter Up" video sound downright reasonable.

The threshold question—whether education and instruction for children under two years old are helpful—is still being asked. And the answer is not good for entrepreneurs who depend on the public's perception that babies are highly educable. The best example of such an entrepreneurial project is Baby Einstein, which remains a popular DVD series despite suffering a major hit to its reputation. Baby Einstein once was the New York Yankees of children's videos. According to one 2003 study, a third of all American babies, from six months to two years old, had seen at least one Baby Einstein video—an astonishing statistic.

Baby Einstein was founded in 1997 by Julie Aigner-Clark, a mom with a toddler and an excellent sense of timing. Five years after starting the company, she sold it to Disney for a reported $25 million. By that time, Baby Einstein had branched out to include books, flashcards, and clothing. The DVDs, filled with bright colors, puppets, and soothing music, had become as indispensible as the sippy cup for most American families. Indispensible, though not necessarily recommended for your baby. In fact, the American Academy of Pediatrics has issued a policy statement objecting to video-watching for children under two. Shortly after the sale of Baby Einstein, Disney began fielding complaints from a children's rights group about its claim that babies watching Baby Einstein videos were learning. They might have been smiling, gurgling, and even crawling. But learning? Ultimately, Disney settled the dispute by offering refunds.

"We see it as an acknowledgment by the leading baby video company that baby videos are not educational, and we hope other baby media companies will follow suit by offering refunds," said Susan Linn, director of the Campaign for a Commercial-Free Childhood, to the *New York Times*.

Just as Aigner-Clark tapped into the dream of brainy babies, other entrepreneurs have focused on baby and toddler athletes. Their ventures fall into three main categories: toddler gyms, play groups, and the rapidly expanding line of baby-sports DVDs.

Toddler Gyms

If you live in the United States, chances are you're within a fifteen-minute drive of one of these. Whether to refer to the activities that go on in these gyms as sports training is open to debate. Often they're more like supervised play, with kids running, jumping, and taking a few tentative steps on a balance beam. On the other hand, if kids are jumping around in a gym, what else would you call it?

By any name, toddler gyms have been a giant business opportunity for adults, from independent coaches to investors on the hunt for the next big score. The national companies have hundreds of locations. One recently opened its doors in mainland China.

What's remarkable about these gym empires is their success in attracting the youngest children. A good example is My Gym, based in Sherman Oaks, California. My Gym got started twenty-five years ago and has since grown to two hundred gyms in the United States and around the world. The video at the My Gym homepage doesn't push the idea that it's a place to groom a sports champion. There is not a single mention of college scholarships or alumni who have graduated from the uneven bars at My Gym to playing center court at Wimbledon.

But there are references, albeit subtle ones, that this is an ideal place to sign up a child with potential for greatness. As the cheerful video on the company site chirps: "Our extraordinary programs and facilities were created to help children six weeks to 13 years of age develop physically, cognitively and emotionally. For over 25 years, young imaginations have soared and children have triumphed at my gym." There are ten My Gyms in Maryland, six in Texas, and forty-two in California. Most customers are very young: 90 percent of the kids who attend My Gym are four and a half years old and under; more than half are under three.

The starting age seemed low. What does a six-week-old do at a gym, I wanted to know? "Not much," says Matt Hendison, who has a good sense of humor. "The reality is it's a mom's class with newborns. The babies get acclimated to sights and sounds." The executive vice president of marketing and entertainment at My Gym, Hendison explains that the classes are as much for moms—often first-time gym goers—as for the newborns. "There's no tumbling. No jumping jacks."

It's pretty much the same story at the Little Gym, which, name aside, is actually larger than My Gym—300 locations worldwide, including Kuwait City, Cairo, and Shanghai. (In fact, the Little Gym is one of the more potent exports that the United States has in China. By 2015, the company expects to have opened a hundred Little Gyms for Chinese parents and kids.)

The first Little Gym opened more than thirty years ago, dreamt up by an educator whose progressive idea was to invite parents to experience the joy of sports with their little kids. In 1992, the company became the Little Gym International Inc. and started selling franchises. To buy one, and to offer the company's lineup of gymnastics, dance, cheerleading, karate, and sports-skills development classes, now costs from $40,000 to $70,000.

The Little Gym's chief executive, Bob Bingham, tells me that 23 percent of children enrolled in its programs in the United States, Canada, and Puerto Rico were two and younger. That was up from 18 percent in 2009.

Bingham explains, "That's probably driven by mothers' and dads' awareness that there is a lot we can do for children two and under, a lot we can teach them." The Little Gym's marketing mantra also contributes. On its website, most of the talk is about play for play's sake and other themes of noncompetitiveness. Still, an audio clip ends with a sentence that blurs the issue. "Best of all," it says, "the lessons [children] learn at the Little Gym will give them the head start they need, laying the foundation for a lifetime of success."

Play Groups

Soccer programs around the country have dropped the age of entry over the years from age seven to age five to, in many communities, age three. One for-profit company, Lil' Kickers, based in Redmond, Washington, is ready to give your child a start in the sport as early as eighteen months. There are fifteen Bunnies for each Bunny instructor. Classes are fifty minutes long, and adults must attend with their children.

What do eighteen-month-olds do on a soccer pitch? Because some are just learning to run, not much. Don Crowe, Lil' Kickers founder and chief executive, puts it this way: "We don't even look at what we do with eighteen-month-olds as a sport. It's an activity."

A typical class might include time for soccer skills like running and kicking and non-soccer stuff like stacking up flexible sports cones. Many kids wear Lil' Kickers–issued uniforms in impossibly small sizes, which adds to the cuteness—and the cost (a full uniform of matching jersey and shorts runs $26). The class is over in forty minutes, leaving ample time for naps, diaper changes, and other essential toddler activities.

There are similar programs around the country, but few as established as Lil' Kickers. A CPA who worked for a Big 8 accounting firm when he started Lil' Kickers in 1999, Crowe has grown the company from four locations in the Seattle area to a hundred in twenty-eight states. In 2010, enrollment topped a hundred thousand, he tells me.

I came away from our conversation with two impressions, both of which Crowe had emphasized during our chat. The first is that, for the youngest kids, Lil' Kickers is a laid-back experience. In various ways, the Lil' Kickers founder conveyed this message. "It's about developing the child, not trying to turn them into the next Pele," he said at one point.

The second impression is that Lil' Kickers has a big task in managing the expectations of parents. Not all parents have unrealistic expectations, of course, but enough do to make that one of the most challenging parts of Crowe's job. Some parents are surprised, even disappointed, he says, that Lil' Kickers isn't more serious. "Some come in thinking it's going to be a high level of soccer at age two."

Baby-Sports DVDs

Baby Goes Pro is a product worth hearing more about for two reasons. The first is its name, more marketing sizzle than a promise of athletic greatness. The second is the celebrity of one of the movers and shakers behind Baby Goes Pro, cofounde Gigi Fernandez, a former professional tennis player. Fernandez knows not only how to become a pro athlete, but how to become a star. Fernandez's professional tennis resume includes these feats: 17 seventeen Grand Slam doubles titles, a number-one ranking in doubles, and two Olympic gold medals for the United States. She's also been inducted into the International Tennis Hall of Fame.

When she quit tennis in 1997, Fernandez launched a new career—actually several of them. Returning to college, she earned an undergraduate degree, acquired her Florida real estate license and picked up a master's of business administration. She and her partner, former professional golfer Jane Geddes, started a family and, in 2009, welcomed twins, Madison and Karson.

Not long after, Fernandez started down the path that became Baby Goes Pro. She wanted her kids to get started in sports early. Very early. "Being a professional athlete, it's important to me that they're active," she tells me. "They're not genetically my kids. So I wanted to do something extra to make sure they were athletic and coordinated children."

Her twins were babies when she began scouring store shelves and surfing the Internet in search of teaching aids. The investigative work turned up a few sports DVDs for children that age, but Fernandez disliked them. "There was one introducing kids to golf that I didn't care for," she says. "It was kids running around a golf course, whacking balls. They had a driver on the putting green."

With a business partner, Fernandez started her company and rolled out the first Baby Goes Pro DVD in 2010. It covers five sports—baseball, basketball, golf, soccer, and tennis—touches on rules and equipment, and features an animated monkey named Emkei.

Nothing about the venture seemed controversial to Gigi Fernandez. Her children had a need, and she thought other families might have a similar need. She came up with a catchy name. She began selling it in stores and on the Baby Goes Pro website. What was the big deal? Of course she wasn't trying to dupe parents into believing their kids would go pro. Are there parents out there dumb enough to fall for a line like that?

Fernandez was patient during our interview, but by the end a note of exasperation had crept in. "We think it's educational and instructional," she tells me. (Does she have any idea the lawyers' fees that Disney racked up making the same claim?) "We're not suggesting your kid will turn pro."

Such talk brings out the cynic in Bob Bigelow. Despite his outgoing nature and infectious laugh, the former pro basketball player and youth sports activist does cynical well. "You're talking to one of the most jaded, sanctimonious people on earth when it comes to this stuff," says the former Ivy League and National Basketball Association player with a laugh.

"This is Baby Mozart stuff: you play Mozart for the baby in utero and it comes out some sort of fine arts major," Bigelow says. "There are millions of American parents worried to death that their children might fall behind somebody else's kid. So the emphasis in youth sports has become more, more, more, younger, younger, younger.

"I am well aware of why entrepreneurs do this. There is money to be made. I'll never deny these folks a chance for that. That said, it is well known in my business that athletic ability comes later not sooner. If they are out there propagating claims that if a baby does this, it will be [a good athlete] and if it doesn't it won't, I am going to put my hand up and say this is crap."

"Why does Fernandez call her company and her DVD Baby Goes Pro?" I ask Bigelow.

He laughs and speaks again about the vulnerability of parents, our genetic predisposition to believe everything when it comes to our children's futures. "What would you expect them to call it?" he asks. "Baby Goes Pre-School?"

I couldn't leave this subject before checking in with Lyle Micheli, whose opinions about sports, kids, and health I greatly value. Micheli is an orthopedic surgeon and founder of the first pediatric sports-medicine clinic in the United States at Children's Hospital in Boston. He treats thousands of kids injured playing on rec fields and high school gyms each year. He literally wrote the book on kids' sports and health, *The Sports Medicine Bible for Young Athletes*.

When I reach Micheli in his office in Boston, I explain that I'm looking into a new youth-sports niche—sports training for babies. There is silence on the other end of the line.

"That's really amazing. What's next?" he says.

I tell him about my conversation with Doreen Bolhuis of Gymtrix and her comment that children who started as babies in her program had success later in sports. In our earlier chat, Bolhuis had told me, "The children we have worked with through thirty years are superstars when they get into middle school and get into sports. They have a broad range of abilities. The parents will come to us amazed, saying, 'My husband and I are klutzes, but the coaches are saying that our kids are so talented.' My response is that they're not talented; they're trained."

Again, silence. Finally, Micheli replies, "I don't know that there is any evidence that training in this infancy stage accelerates coordination and response time."

I replayed Bolhuis's comments about babies being cooped up by the adults, "containerized," as she put it. Was that an argument for formalized baby fitness? I asked.

"Kids naturally will be active," he says.

My ten minutes with Micheli were about up. It was clear that he was not yet sold on the idea of sports classes and videos for babies. Before rushing off to his clinic for a day of treating injured athletes, he laughs and says, "We won't be putting their brochures in our clinic."

For my part, the journey into sports training for babies had confirmed some assumptions and dispelled others. More than ever, I was convinced that the product being sold by most entrepreneurs is hope, much of it misplaced. As long as we dream for our kids, there will be entrepreneurs launching companies such as Baby Goes Pro and Gymtrix.

I spoke with lots of people involved in many aspects of the sports-training-for-babies industry—except the babies. The interviews with parents were for the most part reassuring. Perhaps they were on guard and censoring their comments. Generally, I found them realistic about what a gym class or a soccer clinic for a toddler might accomplish—and what it wouldn't. Often, a parent's goal was to find an activity out of the house that his child could do with other children. Many said that the best activity would be one that allowed their kids to blow off so much energy that they would come home ready for a nap.

Lisa Mullen was typical of these parents. When I spoke with her, she'd recently visited several children's gyms in the Baltimore area in hopes of finding "a physical outlet" for her high-energy son. She expressed no interest in grooming sixteen-month-old Michael for a college soccer scholarship. The gym she chose won her over for its low-key atmosphere and varied activities. During the first class, Michael and his two classmates swung from a bar, walked on a low balance beam, and banged drumsticks. "They're trying to promote listening skills and following directions as well as socialization with other kids," she tells me.

Technically, these activities are sports training for toddlers. Yet they seem entirely reasonable.

For me, the question with regard to these companies was not what they were selling as much as what parents were led to believe they were buying. The companies pitching fun, socialization, and an afternoon outing for baby were delivering exactly what they'd promised.

At the other end of the spectrum is Doreen Bolhuis, a sincere, earnest fitness pro who believes that babies in a sense are athletes-in-training. More than a year after the *Times* ran my article about her company, I've been unable to find a physician who sees the benefits of sports training for toddlers as Bolhuis does, though apparently there are like-minded politicians. Recently I stumbled onto an announcement from the Doreen's home state of Michigan: she had just been appointed to the Governor's Council on Physical Fitness, Health, and Sports.

THREE

Youth Sports, USA

Round Rock, Texas, may not be a place you've heard a lot about. Or heard of period. But the little city off Interstate 35 north of Austin has quite a bit going for it. It is the hometown of Dell computers, which has a sprawling complex here and a workforce of 6,600. It is the hometown of Juarez Restaurant and Bakery, which makes the best tamales you've ever tasted. And Round Rock is the Sports Capital of Texas.

It's a big claim and, inconveniently for Round Rock, not supported by all the facts. Texas is home to two Major League Baseball franchises, two National Football League teams, and three entries in the National Basketball Association—none located in Round Rock. Texas Christian University is a rising collegiate football power, and the University of Texas is a long-established one. Neither plays here.

Round Rock does have a sports legacy, though. A few decades ago, the city bought about 570 acres of rolling property on the edge of town. Slowly, it has pulled off a magical transformation, remaking Old Settlers Park into a kids' sports paradise. There are traditional areas of the park—walking trails, pastoral picnic groves, a hundred-acre fishing hole. Then there is the temple to youth—soccer pitches, tennis courts, beach-volleyball pits, a Frisbee golf course, and, most impressively, a startling layout of five softball and twenty baseball fields.

The sports venues have gone up in stages as the city's plan to become a youth sports tourism center has taken shape. Sharon Prete, the city's former recreation and parks director, remembers the quizzical reaction of some locals when they learned their tax dollars were being spent for groomed ball fields for out-of-town youth players. "There was a letter to the editor about the Taj Mahal that I was building out there," says Prete. "It was one of those local little jabs that irritated me at the time."

Then, as now, Prete didn't approve of the parent-driven direction that youth sports were headed in. "The pressure on four- and five-year-olds to be on select teams is ridiculous. I am exaggerating a little, I realize. But there are a certain amount of dads who just know their child is 'the one.'"

Still she and other city leaders were convinced they were on the trail of something important for the economy of Round Rock. "Today, youth sports are a chaperoned, organized activity," Prete says. "A sports tournament becomes a summer vacation. It's relatively inexpensive. Everyone gets out of town."

About ten years ago, Round Rock plowed a lot more money into youth sports. It hired a marketing agency to help it sharpen its pitch to youth sports groups. That investment delivered the city's tongue-in-cheek claim to being the Sports Capital of Texas; a slick website, Sportscapitaloftexas .com; a Round Rock catchphrase, Game On!; and a splashy logo, one of those ubiquitous fold-up chairs found on sidelines at kids' games—this one with a Texas state-flag motif.

Marilyn Porter is impressed. She's a sprightly grandmother from Franklin, Louisiana, here in Round Rock in late July for a girls' softball tournament. She's standing behind the bench at Richardson Field (named for softball legend Dot Richardson) and marveling at the acres of diamonds. "The whole facility here is one of the best we've seen," she tells me.

That was no idle compliment. The summer we met, Porter had seen dozens of softball games at parks from Panama City, Florida, to Vicksburg, Mississippi. Her granddaughter, eight years old, was the starting third baseman for the Louisiana Fusion, a team that was set to play seventy games that summer. By the time I caught up with the Fusion in Round Rock, the team had already had been on eleven road trips.

"The parents love softball," Porter says. "And the girls do too, of course."

How the Fusion ended up so far from home on this particular July weekend explains a lot about the central place that youth sports occupy in the lives of many families—and the costs that parents willingly bear. That weekend, the Fusion was supposed to be in Gulfport, Mississippi, for a tournament of "travel select" teams, the level for the most talented, most competitive players. The parents loved that tournament and loved those fields in Gulfport. "The fields looked like greens on a golf course. The buildings looked like clubhouses," Marilyn Porter tells me.

It took a manmade disaster to keep them away. This was the summer of the Gulf Coast oil spill. All hands were needed in Gulfport to fight the disaster, so the girls' softball tournament was cancelled.

"You should have seen the girls' faces when they found out we weren't going to Gulfport. They were crying," Marilyn Porter says. A month later, the Fusion girls were sports tourists in Round Rock.

No doubt, youth sports have been good for Round Rock. Good as in highly efficient in generating money and creating jobs. Most years, thirty thousand to forty thousand children converge on the city with big equipment bags and bigger dreams. They're accompanied by an entourage of parents, grandparents, big brothers, and little sisters, all ready to spend. Local shopping malls are jammed. Restaurants are busy. In less than two decades, the number of local hotels has gone from four to twenty-four. Tax on hotel rooms alone nets the city $30 million a year.

"It's pretty exciting to go to a restaurant on the weekend, all these kids, all ages, everyone in uniform. You can hardly get in anywhere to eat," says Mike Robinson, a former mayor of Round Rock. "It frustrates some of the locals, all the waiting for tables and traffic. But I tell them that it's all good, because it means people are in town spending money."

The boom in youth-sports tourism isn't confined to this enterprising town. It's a national phenomenon involving dozens of communities and some of the biggest brands in pro sports and kids' entertainment. Is that positive for children?

Anything that promotes togetherness between parents and children would figure to be a plus. The same goes for activities that encourage kids to play with and learn from their peers. But turning kids' sports into a summer-long road trip distorts and diminishes youth sports, changing them in ways that we rarely talk about. The more miles we travel, the more money we spend, the more time we invest crisscrossing the country, the more we expect from the experience and from our kids. It isn't enough simply to be on the team. It isn't enough just to have fun. The unspoken, and often unintended, message from parents to kids can be that they have to *deliver* to make that summer of sacrifice worthwhile. Often we're not keen on talking about this or even aware that it might be a part of the calculus of youth sports. But it's a fact of life every bit as real as last night's box score.

Dan Vaughn, who runs one of the biggest events of the summer in Round Rock, the PONY national girls' softball tournament, sees parents struggling to keep their ambitions in check all too often. "Most of our issues are with the loud parents," he tells me. "Unfortunately, you have quite a few living their lives through the kids."

When did youth sports become a tourism dynamo? And why? As late as the 1970s, the idea that children would spend multiple weeks each summer playing in sports tournaments that required hours of travel and nights spent in hotels would have been met with disbelief. There were exceptional cases. In the 1940s, an annual kids' football game, the Santa Claus Bowl, drew youth teams from across the country to Lakeland, Florida, as much for the warm sun as for the action on the field. The Little League World Series has been a gathering place for youth baseball players going back to the days of the Santa Bowl. The annual kids' tournament, now an iconic sports spectacle that stretches over eleven days, started in Williamsport, Pennsylvania, in 1947 as a friendly competition among twelve leagues from neighboring towns (eleven from Pennsylvania, one from New Jersey). A year later, Little Leaguers from St. Petersburg, Florida, entered the tournament. In the 2010 Little League World Series, the Arabian American Little League of Dhahran, Saudi Arabia, played the Fu-Hsing Little League of Kaohsiung, Chinese Taipei. It's also a highly visible media event—in 2011, nearly seventy Little League games were broadcast on regional and national TV in the month of August alone.

But youth sports remained a mostly local affair, played in backyards and on neighborhood rec fields, into the 1970s. In the youth-sports survey that I conducted, there was an echo of that. One of the questions I posed was: When you were a child, what is the farthest you traveled to participate in a sports meet or game? Half said they'd never traveled for sports or, if they had, not more than fifty miles. Just 19 percent said they'd traveled a hundred miles or more.

That has changed. Now, by the time a child is nine or ten, chances are she has had some exposure to (aptly named) travel sports. For three to four months, sometimes longer, players and parents are on a seemingly perpetual road trip, driving to courts and fields in towns they barely knew existed. This is a prelude to the weekend trips that take teams even farther from home, sometimes hundreds of miles, and require families to spend a weekend shuttling their children from the gym or pool to the nearest Day's Inn or Best Western.

Some parents genuinely enjoy the experience, considering it valuable family time. Others condition themselves not to think too deeply about something that may be mildly objectionable but over which they seem to have little control. And then there are parents like Andrew Zimbalist, who, despite their abiding love of sports and their children, wonder how they got themselves into this mess.

Zimbalist, a professor of economics at Smith College, has written extensively about the business of sports. He lives in western Massachusetts with his wife and family, including Max Zimbalist, an eager twelve-year-old soccer player. Max plays for a local travel team that, in search of competition, roams great distances. A few times a year—in fact, on several consecutive weekends–the team hits the road to play opponents on Cape Cod, 150 miles away.

Mind you, Andy Zimbalist is observing, not complaining. Okay, he's complaining a little. But the long drives have given him time and reason to ponder the situation. "The parents are spending money, of course. There's the gas, which, if you were getting reimbursed, would be something like fifty cents a mile. You're stopping for food. And if it's a two-day deal, there's a night at a hotel," Zimbalist says. "To me, the story also is how much of a time investment there is. Time is valuable both to the kids and the parents. It means we're not engaging in other forms of leisure, not doing productive work. As a parent, maybe you go to work on Monday exhausted."

It's impossible to say how many families are on the same travel-sports treadmill. But the number clearly is growing. In my business-of-youth-sport survey, I again saw a sign. After asking the parents about their travel patterns as youth players themselves, I followed up with an almost identical question focused on a younger generation: "What is the farthest your child has traveled to participate in a sports meet or game?" Over half said more than a hundred miles.

When did youth sports tourism begin to take shape as a full-blown industry? That's also hard to pinpoint. Not only for me, but for Don Schumacher, who qualifies as an expert in the field. Schumacher heads a Cincinnati-based organization called the National Association of Sports Commissions. He also runs a consulting firm that advises communities seeking to attract youth sports tournaments. Until the early 1990s, he tells me, few people looked at youth sports as having much to do with tourism. They were just, well, youth sports. Then more tournaments began to pop up, and communities began to see financial opportunity. Schumacher ticks off a list of towns that were early to the party: Panama City, Florida; Virginia Beach, Virginia; Kingsport, Tennessee; Rockford, Illinois; Frisco and Round Rock, Texas.

"That's just the tip of the iceberg," Schumacher says, listing another dozen small towns that have made big investments in youth sports more recently.

Private investors are also jumping in. The population of

Cooperstown, New York, home of the Baseball Hall of Fame, swells each summer when the gates open to Dreams Park, a maze of ball fields that bills itself as "America's First and Foremost Youth Baseball Experience." In Aberdeen, Maryland, sports legend Cal Ripken Jr. has created a baseball kingdom for small people with kid-sized replica stadiums of Oriole Park at Camden Yards, Wrigley Field, and Fenway Park. And in a category all its own is the ESPN Wide World of Sports Complex at Disney World, a paradise for children with almost any sports passion.

The 220-acre campus outside Orlando includes two field houses; a 9,500-seat ballpark; eight all-purpose outdoor fields; four baseball diamonds; six softball diamonds; a track and field complex; a cross-country course; and ten tennis courts, including an 8,500-seat stadium court where contestants at center court have included Serena Williams.

Disney opened the park in 1997, and over the next twenty years, estimates that more than 2 million kid players will have vacationed there. Disney is able to sustain the numbers largely due to a partnership with the largest youth sports organization in the United States, the Amateur Athletic Union. Each year, the AAU sponsors 250 national championships in myriad sports and holds as many as seventy at Disney World. It's true that some kids would play soccer all day and night if their parents let them. Because most don't allow that, Disney profits again when the kids line up for admission to its other Orlando theme parks.

Disney officials claim not to know how many sports customers are swiping their credit cards at other spots around the park. But Ken Potrock, senior vice president of Disney Sports Enterprises, told *USA Today*, "One thing we do know is that 85% of people coming here to compete would not have come to Disney World otherwise."

Former Baltimore Oriole great Cal Ripken's baseball complex in Aberdeen, Maryland, is the same sort of kids' paradise, minus Donald Duck and Goofy. Aberdeen is a stout, working-class town. For almost a hundred years, the city's main calling card and major employer has been a military installation, the Aberdeen Proving Grounds. The Army tests hardware here before it is pressed into service in Iraq and other theaters of operation. That military connection has been overshadowed of late by Aberdeen's status as the hometown of Ripken. A baseball Hall of Famer, Ripken was a principled, hard-working player credited by many with having rescued baseball after a management lockout cancelled the 1994 World Series, alienating millions of fans.

Ripken's dream for his post–playing days had been to build a baseball city for children. Even before he quit baseball, after the 2001 season, he began laying the foundation. If you had been driving on Interstate 95 north of Baltimore in those days, you would have seen it sprouting out of the ground next to the highway. In addition to the city's facsimile stadiums of Camden Yards, Fenway Park, and Wrigley Field, which are quite accurate and very cool, the complex includes a 5,500-seat minor-league ballpark called Ripken Stadium, a hotel, and a conference center.

Ripken's dream was also a for-profit business. His family members are owners of the Aberdeen Ironbirds, a Class-A baseball team affiliated with Ripken's former ballclub, the Baltimore Orioles. The combination of the attractive stadium and celebrity owner has turned the Ironbirds into a major success, if not on the field then always at the ticket office. Sellouts at Ripken Stadium are not unusual.

The youth-sports wing of the Ripken campus also has generated buzz. Each summer, hundreds of youth teams converge on Aberdeen to play in tournaments. Some drive hours for the chance to breathe the Ripken air and play on the best fields that they've ever seen. As the Ripken Tournaments website explains, there are thrills waiting for the whole family:

> Become a big leaguer at age 10: Hit a homerun over the Green Monster at Fenway Park, slide into second on the Polo Grounds, or even swing for the Warehouse at Oriole Park at Camden Yards. Get your heart racing as you hear over the PA system: "At bat, Number 8. . . ." Coaches can make calls from big league dugouts and glance over at the professional scoreboards.

When money is no object, there's also the Ripken Experience Camp, a weeklong, please-don't-wake-me-up adventure that features personal instruction from the Hall of Famer and a workout at a major-league ballpark. The price? $1,495. But hey, it's your child. (Full disclosure: A few summers ago, it was *my* child!)

The baseball complex was a costly project, one that seemingly would be a great boost for Aberdeen but far too ambitious for the little city (population 14,000) to pay for. The estimated price of the project was $25.5 million, and a plan was arrived at to share the cost among the parties that stood to gain the most: the State of Maryland ($7.5 million), the City of Aberdeen ($5 million), Harford County ($2 million), and Ripken's business entity, the Tufton Group ($11 million).

Aberdeen's financial commitment was sizable. But how many chances like this would come along for the little town to step into the limelight, to steer millions of tourism dollars to its coffers? City leaders came up with a plan to pay off the money to build Ripken Stadium. Next door to the proposed ballpark was city-owned land that would now be in a prime location. On the parcel, they envisioned a $65 million sports-themed shopping complex crowded with fans drawn to Aberdeen by the minor league games and Ripken's youth tournaments and camps. The taxes raised from the movie theaters, restaurants, and shops would cover the city's debt service each year until all the money was paid off. That's how the plan was supposed to work. And it might have— if the shopping mall had been built. But there were delays. Then the bottom dropped out of the economy and the developer lost interest. Eight years later, the first signs of commercial development are appearing—at last.

In 2009, Aberdeen's total budget was $12.4 million. Its obligation for Ripken Stadium was another $706,000— money it didn't have. City leaders met with Ripken's officials to see if the baseball hero's company might buy the stadium, but those discussions faltered. There's been talk of levying a new hotel tax, but that hasn't happened either. Meanwhile, Aberdeen's financial hole deepens.

"We took a gamble and thought it was a gamble worth taking and it kind of backfired on us," Doug Miller, Aberdeen's city manager, told the *Baltimore Business Journal* about the plan to count on amusement taxes to pay back the stadium debt. "Hence we're here with a bad deal and that's not Ripken's fault."

It's a cautionary tale that politicians in Mooresville, North Carolina, are heeding—to a point. The small town is about to become an epicenter of youth baseball. In a year, thousands of families will be decamped there, dropping their money in local hotels and restaurants. Jobs will be easier to come by, especially low-paying ones for desk clerks, maids, and managers at fast-food establishments. Real estate speculators likely will fare well: properties values are expected to shoot up, especially for the parcels around the baseball village, where the new restaurants and budget hotels will be built.

But like the good folks of Aberdeen, the taxpayers of Mooresville will be taking a financial leap with limited options should the project fail to live up to heady expectations. To lure the project to their community, Mooresville and Iredell County each contributed $500,000 over ten years to the project. The Mooresville Convention and Visitors Bureau kicked in another $1.2 million. And there will be other costs to the public, such as upgrading the roads around the project. In summers to come, they may be traveled by as many as eighty thousand visitors.

To their credit, local politicians seemed to be going into the project with open eyes.

"Any time you do something different there's a chance you could be wrong," Iredell County Commissioner Ken Robertson said when the deal was announced. The developers of the baseball complex are "going to build it, but there's no guarantee that people will come," he said.

Or that they will come to your town. The first communities and resorts to become destinations for youth-sports tourism now have plenty of company. And each year dozens more localities, eyeing the success of established programs in places like Round Rock and Disney World, plot ways to capture a piece of the pie. Mankato, Minnesota, hired a consultant to assess its tourism weaknesses and strengths (central location for Midwest events, a thousand hotel rooms). South Bend, Indiana, leverages its luster as the home of Notre Dame football. "When people come to town for a sporting event, which is really the hot industry right now— these youth sporting tournaments—the grandparents come, the aunts and uncles, it kind of becomes the substitute summer vacation right now for a lot of these folks," the head of the local tourism board told the *South Bend Tribune*. As more Mankatos and South Bends enter the fray, competition for youth sports–tourism dollars stiffens. More communities are bidding for soccer and lacrosse tournaments. More money is being spent to upgrade gyms and build new ones. The pressure to stake out territory, to maintain market share grows each year. In that sense, it's quite different than investing in a professional sports franchise. The owners of pro teams are shielded from competition in their backyards because their leagues often operate as de facto monopolies. The owner of the National Basketball Association team in Cleveland has no worries about a competing team selling tickets forty miles down the road in Akron. The NBA controls how many franchises are awarded and where they do business. The league wouldn't allow it.

In the brave new world of youth sports tourism, it's every woman—or community—for herself. Today's virgin territory may be a sports-tourism battleground tomorrow. Andrew Zimbalist, the noted sports economist, tells me, "If Hilltown, Texas, does it and makes a lot of money, what's to stop Austin, Texas, from doing the same thing?"

I wanted to visit Round Rock when lots of families would be visiting and see kids playing on the field, their younger siblings lined up at the snack bar, and their parents sitting under umbrellas, cheering and coaching. I conferred with Nancy Yawn, director of the visitors bureau, about several possibilities. Each time we spoke, Nancy ended the conversation with a suggestion: 'If you want to be here for a really big tournament, come on down the last week of July."

It turned out to be a mild understatement. The scene at the 2010 PONY Nationals Softball Tournament was young and overwhelmingly female. Take away the metal bats and it could have been a Justin Bieber concert. The tournament is one of the major girls' softball competitions of the summer. PONY is a huge organization, on a scale with the major brands in youth sports. Since its start in 1976, it has grown to four thousand teams in the United States, and girls are playing PONY softball in twenty foreign countries.

The weekend I was there, for the Nationals Tournament, 143 teams had gathered in Round Rock. Each team had ten to fifteen players, and it was a safe bet that at least one parent or supervising adult had attended with each player. Many players came with larger entourages—two parents, grandparents, siblings, and other devoted fans. Doing the math, I estimated 2,100 to 2,400 players in town for the tournament. As for fans, that was anyone's guess—maybe another 10,000. Or double that.

One possible reason for the impressive turnout in Round Rock was the gender of the players. Girls' sports tournaments consistently draw more family members than boys' tournaments, according to an article in the *New York Times*.

"There are far more people who will travel with 12-year-old girls than even 12-year-old boys. And vastly more people will travel with 12-year-old girls than 18-year-old boys," Don Schumacher told *Times* reporter Katie Thomas.

Mika Ryan, president of the Mercer County Sports and Entertainment Commission in New Jersey, concurred, telling the *Times* that her group specifically targets girls' events. "It's not like parents love their sons any less, but it is a phenomenon that you see happening," she said.

In Round Rock, I found lots of families revved up about girls softball. And I found this by checking out their trucks and minivans. In my years covering sports at high school fields and pro arenas, I have seldom dawdled in parking lots. The PONY national tournament was a little different, because the action—at least some of it—was in the parking lot. Lots around the fields were jammed with pickups, SUVs, and minivans. Each vehicle told a story, some more legibly than others.

On virtually every car, windows were decorated with slogans, victory chants, ditties. The car next to mine had a big message scrawled on the back window in pink and orange that announced: "This vehicle won't stop—It goes all the way." Going along the row of vehicles, I paused at a Ford Expedition, pulled out my Flip camera, and pointed it at a message in curvy green script: "Don't you wish you hit like a girl?"

When I saw the ballfields at Old Settlers Park, I did wish I hit like a girl. This is the major leagues for kids' sports. Imagine the spring training headquarters of the Los Angeles Dodgers, only a lot of the players are nine. And half are girls. The fields are manicured and beautiful. Many are framed by stone and concrete grandstands with sun roofs. The fields are laid out in clusters. From the concourse behind the home plate of one field you can often catch the action on two others. Try that at Yankee Stadium.

When I arrived, there were eighteen games in progress. Eighteen! That's a typical level of activity. Over five days at the PONY tournament, there were five hundred games. I wandered among a cluster of five fields called the Champions Complex, watching young girls bat and field under a blazing sun and watching as the adults reached into coolers and fanned themselves. The games were every bit as serious as the team nicknames: Riptide, Fusion, Blaze, Hotshotz, Mean Machine, Trouble, and Lady Biscuits (take my word for it, don't mess with the Biscuits).

I had come here to follow the money, so that's what I did. One of the first people I wanted to see was Dan Vaughn, the PONY tournament director. Vaughn started coaching in PONY more than thirty years ago, when his daughter was in the program. He's been coming to the national tournament for the last twenty years. I found him in a window-less concrete room behind the snack bar. Sitting next to him was an assistant who seemed to be monitoring the progress of several games and seldom looked up from his laptop.

We talked about all the money sloshing around Round Rock during tournament week. Dan estimated that PONY leaguers occupied as many as 1,500 hotel rooms. (Round Rock has 24 hotels and a startling 2,600 rooms.) The stadium complex we were in had been built with a 13 percent bed tax collected on those rooms. Six percent of that revenue goes to the state and the other seven percent belongs to Round Rock, which helped pay the $18.4 million price tag for this dazzling baseball and softball complex.

Among the tourists occupying one of those hotel rooms was Marilyn Porter. The energetic grandmother was on the road chaperoning the Louisiana Fusion, including her granddaughter, Kailyn Bene Briley. I spoke with Porter and several other parents and grandparents about the fun and seriousness of travel/select softball, and about how these eight-year-olds were on a different level than the average kid player.

"The competition is nothing compared to Rec ball. You go out and watch a Rec team, then you go and watch travel—no comparison," Porter says. "Our team is ranked number two out of twenty-seven teams in the state of Louisiana. In the national USFA [US Fastpitch Association], we're five out of two hundred and nine teams." One girl on the team made the trip despite a case of inflamed adenoids. Her doctor had recommended surgery to remove them—but agreed to postpone the operation until the Fusion's big week in Round Rock. The tournament was that important.

I asked about expenses for softball; Porter estimates that parents spend $4,000 to $5,000 a year. For the Round Rock trip, she anticipated her bill for the week at $1,000 to $1,200. "I always pay cash for everything," she tells me.

This tournament was about more than money. There were teams from many parts of the country, from as close as Round Rock and as far away as California and Puerto Rico. There were teenagers and girls who'd just turned seven. Some teams came from wealth and were well accustomed to travel; others were leaving their hometowns for the first time.

Juan Garcia of Laredo, Texas, is the coach of a determined group of girls called the Laredo All-Stars, which included his twelve-year-old daughter, Dulce. The Laredo All-Stars were doing well enough in the tournament—they'd won a few games. But Coach Garcia explained that the tournament served first as a window to the world outside Laredo, one that was new and exciting for his girls. The day of the opening ceremonies, the Laredo girls mingled with players from a Puerto Rican team and were intrigued "to hear girls with other accents," Garcia says. The next day, it rained. Other teams were upset but not Garcia's. "In Laredo, to get a day of rain, we have to pray for it. Our girls came outside and danced."

I wish I had been standing on the infield dirt of one of the Round Rock diamonds to observe that moment of unscripted fun. It's the kind of scene that gives me hope that in small measure kids' sports may still belong to kids. Let's not be grinches here. Kids playing sports is positive. Kids expanding their worlds through sports is better.

Are those positives what's behind the boom in youth sports tourism? If you believe that, I have some real estate to sell you in Mooresville, North Carolina, or perhaps Aberdeen, Maryland.

FOUR

The Sponsorship Game

Snowboarding is a sport for kids who function perfectly well with two feet on the ground—or none. The repertoire of an accomplished boarder would include the Air and the Fakie (an airborne, 180-degree turn) to the Backside 720 (two full, gravity-defying spins) and other acrobatic moves utterly unfamiliar to anyone over the age of forty. Snowboarders like that their sport isn't entirely accessible. And, after a day on the mountain, they like the feel of carbonated caffeine on their tongues and in their throats. So it's never a surprise to find a kid in a helmet and goggles drinking Mountain Dew.

Snowboarding and skateboarding (its warm-weather twin) have hitched their wagons to Mountain Dew as closely as any sports and consumer brands. For years, the most competitive pro events in action sports have been organized into the summer and winter "Dew Tours." The Dew name and Dew's edgy green-and-red logo are splashed all over mountains and skate parks. And they're just as visible for fans taking in the action on their flat-screen TVs. Twice each hour, there's a break in the action for a Dew commercial. The tours themselves are owned in part by Mountain Dew.

What amounts to ownership of two vibrant, youth-oriented sports does not come cheaply. In fact, PepsiCo,

Mountain Dew's parent, is one of the most prolific spenders on sports among consumer brands. In 2009, the soda and snack-food giant rang up $92 million on sports promotion efforts, according to the *Sports Business Journal*. (In comparison, Nike spent just $58 million.) About $5 million of that each year buys Mountain Dew its toehold in action sports.

Bill Carter's job is to convert those marketing dollars into tens of millions in sales. Carter is a founder and one of the chief creative minds behind Fuse Marketing, a much-respected and highly specialized sports-marketing firm. Fuse is located a little off the beaten track (in Winooski, Vermont) in a slightly unusual office (featuring a private skate park). But perhaps the most distinctive thing about Fuse is the corner of the marketing world it occupies. The thirty-five-person agency specializes in campaigns that leverage youth sports. More precisely, Fuse toils in a specialty within a specialty: action sports, the sliver of fun and games that includes motocross and, yes, skateboarding and snowboarding. The Mountain Dew account is one of Fuse's oldest and most lucrative.

Carter is a nice guy with an informal, self-assured, yet self-deprecating manner. He doesn't rattle easily, and he handles pointed questions without going into a defensive crouch. That was good, because I had come to Winooski to ask him an impertinent question: "Did he really think that what his agency was doing was good for kid athletes?"

Mountain Dew isn't exactly health food. It's high in high-calorie corn syrup and higher in caffeine (according to one online survey, the 55 milligrams in a bottle of Dew ranks the drink alongside nerve-jangling choices like Red Bull and Jolt). And it isn't exactly recommended in a program to promote dental health. One Kentucky dentist went on *Good Morning America* to talk about the $150,000 he'd invested in a mobile clinic so he could fix the teeth of rural kids rotted by Mountain Dew and drinks like it.

Carter didn't need a lecture from me about the product's health value. I simply asked him whether you could be a friend of youth sports and an advocate for Mountain Dew at the same time.

Carter thought for a moment, looked away, and then straight at me. "It's not lost on anyone in this office that, while we're helping our clients communicate with the youth market, not all the products that we work on are entirely healthy," he says. "To no one's surprise, soda isn't entirely healthy. Beef jerky [a product also pitched by Fuse] isn't entirely healthy.

"I don't see it as a negative to acknowledge the truth, and the truth is that teenagers shouldn't be drinking soft drinks or eating certain snacks in anything but a moderate way. If I thought we were going over the top, and promoting something unhealthy, I don't see how we could participate. We wouldn't do the work."

A few weeks earlier, I'd been sitting across a table from the sports sociologist Jay Coakley, one of the most respected and outspoken thinkers in his field, and had gotten a different perspective. Coakley told me he did not see any justification for the way that Corporate America "preys" upon youth sports. The idea that consumer brands were using kids' play to pitch products that might compromise their health clearly galled him.

"To me, it's morally indefensible," he says. "I know the rationalization: these marketing campaigns aren't telling kids to live on Mountain Dew. They can eat granola with it if they want. It's up to the parents to set limits. And if they don't, it's the parents' fault."

The whole thing clearly frustrates Coakley. "We live in

a culture where no one gives a damn about the common good," he says.

Corporate America embraces youth sports for reasons that are best described as pragmatic: it's where the money is—lots of it. Assigning a dollar figure to the youth sports economy is challenging because it's nearly impossible to define what's meant by the youth sports economy. It's soccer cleats, volleyball nets, and racing swimsuits, of course. Is it also the sports video games that are as popular with kids as the sports themselves? If so, then what about the computer console your child uses to play that game? Or the multiple packages of microwave popcorn consumed as kids sit in front of the TV? In 2010, the *Columbus Dispatch* ran an excellent series on the overheated state of youth sports. Citing figures reported "by nonprofit sports groups to the IRS," the newspaper put the figure at $5 billion a year.

The number of human beings engaged in playing, coaching, cheering, and agonizing over youth sports is easier to count. According to the Sporting Goods Manufacturers Association, the United States is home to 25 million basketball players, 14 million soccer players (during the outdoor season alone), and 7.6 million tackle football players. Baseball adds 15 million. Gymnastics kicks in almost 4 million participants.

Behind each player is a cadre of parents, coaches, and just plain fans with billions in disposable income. This explains, if explanation is needed, the robust corporate-sponsorship programs of major youth sports organizations. The Amateur Athletic Union, the largest of all national kids' sports programs, counts close to two dozen national sponsors in its corner, including a Major League Baseball team (the Tampa Bay Rays), a women's professional league (the Women's National Basketball Association), and a hotel chain that "leaves the light on." At last count, Little League Baseball's bench was almost as deep, with a fast-food chain, sporting-goods retailer, lighting supplier, and a leading brand of sunflower seeds among its sponsors.

The question isn't whether corporate sponsors have billions of dollars riding on youth sports—they do. Rather, it's "Are there consequences for children?"

Businesses have been underwriting youth sports for nearly as long as kids have been playing in organized leagues. The practice dates back seventy years at least—to the birth of Little League Baseball.

In his autobiography, *A Promise Kept,* Little League founder Carl Stotz recalls that businesses helped launch his kids' sports enterprise in 1939. The Great Depression was on, and the reasons for spending scarce extra money on a startup kids' league in Williamsport, Pennsylvania, weren't obvious. Stotz tells of approaching fifty-seven businesses before the first owner finally wrote out a check. It came from his boss at the Lundy Lumber Company, where Stotz was a bookkeeper. Eventually, two other local merchants stepped forward—owners of Lycoming Dairy and Jumbo Pretzel. Each paid thirty dollars to support the league. Their sponsorship was a gift to their communities. Corporate backing of youth sports came later. Again, Little League was an early adopter.

By 1948, the organization had spread to nearly a dozen states, and each August hosted a national tournament (later, the Little League World Series). Stotz needed funds to offset the travel expenses of teams coming from distant leagues to the small town in the mountains of central Pennsylvania. His solution, though he likely wouldn't have called it that, was to strike a deal with a corporate sponsor. For $5,000 he sold the tournament naming rights to U.S. Rubber, then a manufacturer of kids' sneakers, and he also threw in advertising space on the kids' uniforms. That year, half the players in the tournament wore uniforms that spelled out "U.S. Keds," and the other half "U.S. Royals."

That sort of advertising must have crossed whatever lines of propriety existed seventy-plus years ago, because the deal has never been repeated. Little Leaguers at the World Series have not worn a company name on their uniforms since. That is not to suggest the corporate sponsors are unwelcome in Williamsport. Decades later, Little League officials continue to show a knack for packaging and repackaging kids' baseball for eager sponsors. Those on Little League Baseball's e-mail Listserv receive at least one reminder a month. A recent e-mail announced a contest in which moms and dads posted messages to a Facebook page revealing "the ways they share their love of *Frosted Flakes* with their kids."

The trophy for the most durable youth-sports marketing idea of all time belongs to the Ford Motor Company. In 1961, the automaker announced a simple promotion it named Punt, Pass & Kick.

The name said it all. Kids across the country competed in the three basic football skills. In each category, the goal was to achieve both distance and accuracy. Throw it long and throw it straight. Kick it across the playground but try not to hook it over the fence.

It was easy to enter PP&K, assuming you met certain requirements. You had to be a boy, of course. Until the 1970s, girls were barred from most organized kids' sports and were especially unwelcome in "boys'" sports like baseball and football. Parents registered their children at the nearest Ford dealership (no iPhone apps in those days). There was no entry fee, other than the elevated blood pressure experienced by some parents as they were greeted in the showroom by a car salesman.

The competition started at a neighborhood rec field. The winners moved on to a county-wide competition, then to a sectional, then a state final, and so on until the best kids in the country were kicking and punting against each other at halftime of an NFL game. The competition mattered a lot to many parents, a statement I make with confidence because I witnessed it with my own family. I was too young or too scared to try out for PP&K in 1964, but in late summer that year, my father, a confirmed Oldsmobile man, went to the Ford dealership to sign up my brother David, older than me by three years.

David was flawless at fielding ground balls in the backyard and pretty good at shooting a basketball. I never thought of him as a football player, and I doubt he did either. Our exposure to football was confined mostly to pickup games with neighborhood kids that revealed our general lack of polish at punting, passing, and kicking. (Fumbling was a family specialty, however.)

But David was undaunted. He entered the tournament mostly out of a ten-year-old's sense of curiosity and adventure, not caring whether he won and proving it by not even picking up a football for days before the big competition. David's minimalist, no-practice approach to the most important football test of his life marked him as the Joe Namath of his era before there was a Namath era—cool, confident, and content to leave the serious training to others. It puzzled our dad. Irked him, too. Here was a fine opportunity for his firstborn son to work hard and perhaps be recognized as one of the top kid athletes in town. Instead, he was in front of the TV watching the new season of *Ozzie and Harriet*.

When the big day arrived, David didn't wait for my mom or dad. He just walked from our house across Monument Street to the closely mown field where the PP&K competition was getting underway. Or should have been. For reasons neither David nor I can recall, if we ever knew, the turnout of young talent that year was underwhelming. It fell short of the numbers needed for tetherball much less a football game. "When they called for the ten-year-olds, it was just me and one other kid," he tells me.

The sparse turnout brought out the best in my brother. He beat the other kid and walked home with a champion's jacket—a handsome blue PP&K model with cool white-leather sleeves. That was one highlight that remains with David to this day. The other is the look on my dad's face—surprised, perplexed, pleased—when David breezed into the house as our town's latest football hero. As David recalls, "Dad clearly thought this would be a humbling learning experience for me—you can't excel without putting in the hard work. Sometimes it's better to be lucky than good."

Punt, Pass & Kick ran under the banner of Ford from 1961 to 1979 when the automaker pulled the plug, citing the program's mounting expense. PP&K disappeared for a dozen years before being revived by Gatorade in 1993. It continues today with yet another corporate sponsor, Pepsi.

Longevity aside, what is noteworthy about Punt, Pass & Kick is its status as a totem to family values. Few kids' sports campaigns have gotten into the heads of Americans the way PP&K did through the 1960s and, to a lesser extent, still does. The explanation lies in the elements of the competition. At its core, PP&K is about kids dreaming the impossible football dream—wending their way through local tournaments, mowing down competition, until they emerge as the top eight-year-old passer or thirteen-year-old punter in the entire country. What could be more American?

PP&K also has the advantage of being the brainchild of three men of legendary marketing and artistic talent: Pete Rozelle, the advertising executive turned commissioner of the National Football League; Lee Iacocca, the can-do corporate cheerleader of the 1980s, father of the Chrysler minivan, and, back then, Ford Motor Company vice president; and Norman Rockwell, who turned slices of American life into classic works of art.

The program drew yawns at first. After Rozelle and Iacocca announced it at a football writers' luncheon in Chicago, one newspaper referred to the program as "punt, pass, and (place) kick," which, though accurate, lacked the catchy rhythm of PP&K. Other media members at the time ignored the program completely. That soon changed as the NFL and Ford publicity engines began to turn. The carmaker ran an ad in the *New York Times* linking the kids' contest to the home-run hitting competition underway between New York Yankees' sluggers Mickey Mantle and Roger Maris. "You get a home run deal on a '61 Ford or Falcon right now!" the ad read. And below it, "Don't forget to register your boy . . ."

Rockwell was commissioned to turn Punt, Pass & Kick into fine art, and that's what he did. In his painting, two football players are pictured side by side in mirrored poses. One could be a Green Bay Packer. He's a grown man in full uniform, his right leg extended so high he could boot a low-flying bird. The second is a young boy, a PP&K kid dressed for a play date with Beaver Cleaver—white T-shirt, cuffed jeans, and laced street shoes.

Rockwell's painting was reproduced on almost everything connected with PP&K—certificates, plaques, and medals among them. You couldn't think of the program without conjuring up that image of the boy and the pro player simultaneously kicking footballs into orbit. I spent a few days trying to locate Rockwell's original artwork, checking with sources familiar with Rockwell collectors, including curators at the Norman Rockwell Museum in Stockbridge, Massachusetts. I wasn't able to track it down. If it's hanging in your home, treat it well. At an auction in 2006, a Rockwell original fetched $15.4 million.

Perhaps it was the Rockwell cachet. Certainly the timing was right—sports and kids were fresh in the collective mind of the nation in 1961, as President Kennedy had recently established the President's Council on Physical Fitness. Regardless, PP&K quickly emerged as a civic duty as much as a clever sales campaign, which, after all, is what it was. That first year, the five winners of the national competition were rewarded with, among other things, a private visit to the White House, where they received signed photos of President Kennedy (he was in Palm Beach, nursing a bad back). Other politicians also hurried to stand in the reflected light of the popular, even vaguely patriotic kids' sports tournament. One year, the governor of Maryland declared a statewide Punt, Pass & Kick Week.

A measure of PP&K's success was the efforts made to replicate it. Over the years, pro leagues in other sports took turns launching programs that attempted to achieve what Ford and the NFL had created. In 1970, the National Hockey League unveiled a pale imitation it called "Skate, Shoot & Score." In the skating part of the contest, the kid players started at center ice, then skated around pylons placed forty yards apart on one goal line before reversing direction and racing to the other goal line. "The idea is to get kids when they're young and make them think in terms of hockey," a league official said at the time. The NHL hoped to land Ford as the sponsor, but never did. Six years later, Coca Cola backed a kids' national soccer tournament called Kick Me, which probably captured how Coke wanted to punish the ad executive who dreamed up the dud of a promotion.

Today, five decades after PP&K began and thirty years

since Ford pulled its sponsorship, the program is still in the news. In 2011, forty finalists assembled at the Georgia Dome to compete in the national final prior to an NFC Divisional Playoff game. Among them was Jayla Medeiros of Kealakekua, Hawaii, a plucky young lady with a ponytail. In the six- and seven-year-old girls division, Jayla proved that little boys aren't the only ones who can punt, winning the title.

A few months before Jayla's big moment, I called Lee Iacocca. He was living in retirement in California, running the Lee Iacocca Foundation, and rarely being asked to recall his role in Punt, Pass & Kick. He was eighty-six years old and had added a few lines to his resume since the early 1960s. This included bringing Chrysler back from the brink in the 1980s, inventing the minivan, and, for a time, reigning as the best-known CEO in America.

Iacocca's memories of PP&K were less than crystal clear. But during our brief conversation, he explained that the program had been a smashing success, exceeding his expectations. Kids loved participating. Dealers loved the customers who funneled through the front door to sign up their children. "And it sold *a lot* of cars," he said.

There is no shortage of modern-day PP&K imitators. In the age of Facebook, Twitter, and YouTube, such campaigns can tap kid athletes on the shoulder without a parent being aware. For example, there is Prince Tennis's Who's Next campaign, which I stumbled onto while researching some facts for this book.

I became one of 32,858 Facebook followers of Who's Next. A few clicks later, I was on YouTube, watching Prince Sports' CEO Gordon Boggis describe his company's excellent rackets—perfect for the tennis prodigy in your family.

After that I steered over to the Who's Next Web portal, where I met a roster of kid chaps who swing Prince rackets. Flipping through a dozen player card–like images of tennis phenoms carrying the Prince banner I settled on a twelve-year-old powerhouse named Usue Arconada, of Argentina. She seemed like a great young lady, and I admired her work ethic while wondering whether this kid does anything but play tennis.

After watching the Usue Arconada video for three or four minutes, I got the sales pitch, Usue explaining her love for her Prince racket "because it gives me more power and it's not that heavy."

Today, there are few places where sponsorship of kids' sports intrudes more than in the public schools. Once, high school gyms and athletic fields were named for the teams that provided the noise and thrills: Colonial Stadium, Cougar Field, or something equally high-school-sports–like. Now school sports venues are named for supermarkets and auto-parts dealers. Sometimes those corporate names can be seen from blocks away because they appear in seven-foot-high blinking letters.

Corporate-naming deals have been common in the professional and college ranks for close to a century. Wrigley Field, the venerable home of the Chicago Cubs, carries the name of the team owner, Phil Wrigley, but also Wrigley's popular chewing-gum brand. In public schools, the idea began catching on in the first decade of the 2000s.

Early sponsorship deals involved high schools with big stadiums and winning traditions, those that attracted large crowds every Friday night or Saturday morning. Before long, sponsors were negotiating with the principals of elementary schools.

Reporter Bill Pennington describes the latter trend in a wonderful, if disturbing, article in the *New York Times*. Featured in the piece is the struggling town of Brooklawn, New Jersey, where school budgets are tight and officials are forever searching to pay for the few extracurricular programs still offered. In 2001, students at Brooklawn's Alice Costello Elementary School arrived for classes one day and noticed something about their old gymnasium had changed. Affixed to the side of the old brick building was a lighted seven-foot sign that read, ShopRite of Brooklawn Center.

The Brooklawn school board had agreed to rename the gym at its cash-strapped schools for a fee of $100,000. According to Pennington, that wasn't the only part of the building being offered as ad space. Also available: the jump circle on the gym floor for $5,000, an ad at the baseline for $2,500, and a wall banner for $500. The school board president, hardly skittish about the program, told the *Times*: "I'm looking into selling advertising on the children's basketball uniforms"—an echo of the Little League World Series misstep more than fifty years earlier.

Brooklawn attracts attention because its palm is out so far. But many schools are playing the same game. Vernon Hills High School outside Chicago built a $1.8 million football stadium in 2002 and paid for it in part by naming the place Rust-Oleum Field. In Texas, the Frisco High School Raccoons play home football games at Pizza Hut Park.

To critics, the suggestion that children benefit from the funds generated by these deals rings hollow. Alex Molnar, a professor of education policy at Arizona State University, told the *Times*, "We have an enormous problem in this country with overweight kids, who have poor diets lacking nutrition, and that contributes to the early onset of diabetes as well. . . . So how is a school district helping that problem by selling Pepsi ads all over the football stadium scoreboard? Why don't they just let Jack Daniels advertise on it, too?"

A product that hasn't elbowed its way into high school sponsorship yet is energy drinks. These drinks, with brand names like Redline, Monster, and Red Bull, are potent stuff. In a can about the size of a cup of Yoplait, they pack a startling dose of stimulant. When it hit the market in 1997, an eight-ounce can of Red Bull contained 80 milligrams of caffeine.

For adults, that's a lot to handle. For kids, regular use of energy drinks can have dangerous, even life-threatening effects. In 2010, ESPN's Tom Farrey told the story of Dakota Sailor, a member of the football team at Carl Junction High School in Missouri. Sailor was just seventeen when he consumed two energy drinks, then, during a practice, suffered a seizure that could have ended his life. The young man's physician told Farrey that the energy drinks had played a "primary role" in the crisis.

In spite of such risks, sales of energy drinks continue to rise, reaching $7 billion in 2010. Ideally, the companies behind these products wouldn't be relying on children for that growth. But that's not clear. The brands do not sponsor mainstream kids' sports—you won't see a Monster energy-drink banner draped poolside at a kids' swim meet. Or a Red Bull banner at a Pop Warner football game. Yet these companies have sponsorship deals with sports leagues and professional athletes who hold sway with young people. Only the most naïve observer would view that as an accident.

The list of such deals increases by the year. For example, Red Bull has had ties with NASCAR and Formula One racing and a center-stage presence in motocross, an action sport for daredevil bicyclists followed closely by teens. Then there's the sports franchise that actually has taken the name of an energy drink—the New York Red Bulls, of Major League Soccer. The Red Bulls' owner: Dietrich Mateschitz, an Austrian billionaire who started the company. The team's new $200 million home field in Harrison, New Jersey? Red Bull Arena of course. How many kids are wearing Red Bulls soccer jerseys? Who can say, though if they purchased an official Juan Agudelo model through the Red Bulls' website, their parents paid $70.45 plus shipping.

Pro athletes on the Red Bull endorsement payroll have included NFL running back Reggie Bush, Olympic beach volleyball gold medalists Todd Rogers and Phil Dalhausser, motocross champion James Stewart, and Olympic skate- and snowboarding legend Shaun White. With his mane of shaggy red hair and take-no-prisoners approach to competition, White is just the sort of athlete that Red Bull presumably seeks. It's impossible to know—and scary to consider—how many kids have reached for a Red Bull, or simply have a favorable impression of the brand, because they associate it with an athlete they admire unconditionally. Clearly, Red Bull believes the numbers are sizable. In 2007, the company signed a three-year deal with White worth more than $1 million a year. In 2011, when the two sides began negotiating a renewal, White's asking price reportedly had leaped to $3 million a year, according to the *Sports Business Journal*.

James Stewart, the motocross champ so revered in his sport that he stars in his own video game, also is on the Red Bull endorsement team. In an interview with ESPN's Farrey, Stewart had no qualms about who was paying him and whether he might indirectly be putting Red Bull in the hands of kids. "I'm sure it's kid-friendly," he said. "When I was a kid I had a lot of energy, so maybe the parents might have something different to say about it, but I'm OK with it." That the Whites and Stewarts of the world—and, notably, the agents who work for them—are prowling for lucrative endorsement deals hardly separates them from other athletes of this or any generation. Since Babe Ruth modeled "All-America athletic underwear" in the 1920s, sports stars have been cashing in on their fame without weighing the consequences (ask former Super Bowl–winning coach Jimmy Johnson about his pitchwork for a male-enhancement firm). Perhaps these sports personalities genuinely are clueless to the health risks of energy drinks.

If there's any doubt that these testimonials filter down to kids, influencing their choices and nudging them toward that first sip of caffeine-in-a-can, look at the video on ESPN.com that accompanied Farrey's excellent piece. The segment shows a scrum of kid athletes pulling and pushing to get their hands on a free can of Monster. At which point one boy states for the camera that energy drinks make him "feel a little bigger, a little older . . . and . . . gimme some pump."

The debate isn't limited to energy drinks. In 2011, sports drinks also came under increased scrutiny. The American Academy of Pediatrics (AAP) issued a case study raising two concerns about Gatorade, PowerAde, and the like. The first is that kids often can't tell the difference between an energy drink and a sports drink. "Some kids are drinking energy drinks—containing large amounts of caffeine—when their goal is simply to rehydrate after exercise. This means they are ingesting large amounts of caffeine and other stimulants, which can be dangerous," said Marcie Beth Schneider, a member of the AAP Committee on Nutrition, in a statement released with the report.

The second concern, as the AAP report notes, is that sports drinks add calories to kids' diets and can contribute to other health problems. And, as the study also notes, except in special cases, the drinks aren't helping kid athletes perform on the field or in the pool.

"For most children engaging in routine physical activity, plain water is best," says Holly Benjamin, another pediatrician and member of the AAP Council on Sports Medicine and Fitness. "Sports drinks contain extra calories that children don't need, and could contribute to obesity and tooth decay. It's better for children to drink water during and after exercise, and to have the recommended intake of juice and low-fat milk with meals."

The sports-drink industry isn't exactly urging us to shut the spigot. Gatorade, for one, spends tens of millions each year on sports marketing. According to the *Sports Business Journal*, the four major American sports leagues—football, baseball, basketball, and hockey—have deals with Gatorade, as do a majority of teams in those leagues. Dozens of star players are paid to pitch the sports drink, including Peyton and Eli Manning, Dwayne Wade, Kevin Garnett, and Landon Donovan. Seventy-four college programs count Gatorade as a sponsor, as do thirteen college conferences and eleven bowl games.

Oh, and Gatorade is a highly visible sponsor of high school basketball tournaments. Next spring, check out the ESPN Rise National High School Invitational presented by Gatorade. I did in March 2011. In a gym in suburban DC, it was me, about 700 fans, and about 700 Gatorade logos plastered on every available surface.

I may be off-base—perhaps water is about to make a comeback as kids' favorite thirst quencher. That would please your kid's doctor. It might not make the Manning brothers happy.

In fairness, the sports drink companies that target kid athletes are following the lead of those that pitch snack chips and sugar-dusted cereals. In a column that underscores this point, Dan Wetzel of *Yahoo Sports* notes that corporate sponsors are fans of their bottom lines first.

Wetzel writes:

You may think this is *just* Little League baseball, but that isn't how the corporations see it.

The Little League game that appears on ESPN and ABC is no different than a Red Sox-Yankees contest, or "Grey's Anatomy" or *SportsCenter*. It is a show designed to sell enough advertising to turn a profit. That's it. That's all. If it wasn't making money, it wouldn't be on the air.

"If Kellogg's (or any other company) didn't think the Little League would help the bottom line, it wouldn't buy in either. No one is in this for their health."

The same pragmatism is evident, even necessary, in the organizations that are advocates for children in and out of sports. Those who speak for children in many forums must weigh the price of their advocacy against the cost of running their programs.

Save the Children is a well-known, nonprofit organization that meets the needs of neglected and impoverished children in more than 120 countries. As its website states, "We help save children's lives, protect them from exploitation and assist them in accessing education and health care."

In 2010, First Lady Michelle Obama was leading a national effort to reduce childhood obesity in the United States. Save the Children stood with her. The organization got behind a campaign to discourage kids' consumption of soft drinks. A number of cities and states around the country—

Mississippi, New Mexico, Washington State, and the District of Columbia, among them—were considering imposing a soda tax. Save the Children favored these measures.

Then suddenly, it didn't. The reversal came as Save the Children was applying for a large grant from Coca Cola to pay for health and education programs in the United States and other countries. When the *New York Times* inquired, Save the Children's chief operating officer said there was no connection between these two facts. Ditto for a $5 million grant that the organization recently had received from PepsiCo.

"We looked at it and said, 'Is this something we should be out there doing and does this fit with the way that Save the Children works?' ... And the answer was no," the Save the Children officer told the *Times*.

Sports sociologist Jay Coakley tells a similar story of perceived influence-peddling. A prominent sports-educators group recently struck a deal with a soft drink company. In the agreement, the association gets funds that it uses to buy and distribute free pedometers to members. The soft drink company receives access to a group of prized educators that it hopes will spread the word about a new brand.

The soda in the middle of the deal was a new diet flavor. So the arrangement wasn't encouraging soda drinkers to consume excess calories. Still, the bargain seemed illogical to Coakley.

"I talk to my friends and they say, 'We know it's a problem, but we couldn't survive without sponsorship. The net result is in our favor.' I buy that to extent," Coakley says. "But when the only money for the public good in this country comes from corporations, it ain't gonna work. The public good is not going to be served."

For the average mom and dad, the effects of corporate

sponsorship are subtle at most. What's the big deal about pulling a jumbo box emblazoned with Tony the Tiger off the supermarket shelf once in a while? Except that every year, kids in America get bigger. They grow into adults more likely than ever to be overweight. That we allow youth sports to be used as a megaphone by companies contributing to the crisis underscores an unhealthy alliance between sports for kids and Corporate America.

Bill Carter of Fuse sports marketing was happy to provide an opposing view. He and I sat across a wide conference table in the Fuse offices in Winooski, Vermont. Just outside the room, his staff of eager artists and writers sharpened campaigns for everything from kids' high-top sneakers to teriyaki-flavored beef jerky.

Did I know much about skateboarding? he asked.

I didn't.

Had I ever heard of the Free Flow Tour? he asked.

I hadn't.

Then he would tell me. The pro skateboard tours go where they crowds are—New York, Boston, Chicago, Portland. The kids in the big cities go to the shows and get to breathe the same air as their heroes. The ones who want to compete can do that too. In the big cities, an amateur skateboarder usually can find a place to compete.

For kids who live far from big cities, it's different, Carter explains. Ten years ago, Mountain Dew asked Fuse to create a tour for amateurs under the age of eighteen at all skill levels and to book events in markets where other skateboard tours never went. It's called the Free Flow Tour. Gatorade took over sponsorship of the tour and spends hundreds of thousands of dollars to keep the tour going.

"If there is no such thing as the Gatorade Free Flow Tour, in those thirty or so markets around the country, there would be nothing to take its place," Carter says. "The kids living in those communities would continue to skate on the street, maybe in a skate park if one exists. They'd have no competition. They do now because that [underwriting such competition] is what corporate interests do best."

That assumes, of course, that the world of kids' skateboarding is better off when adults are guiding the sport, organizing competitions, prescribing rules, and so on. It's an assumption that we make about youth sports at all levels, typically without input from the kids we're organizing for.

But I'd interrupted Bill Carter.

"So I say to sociologists," Carter continues, "I challenge you to fill the void. Show me how you'll pay for youth programs that cost more than the recreation council down the street can raise from parents. Bottom line is, I support corporate interests in youth sports, even though I know it is not entirely positive."

Bottom line is, the adults are in charge.

FIVE
Exposed and Overexposed

Signs of commercialization in youth sports can be subtle, or they can be bold and audacious.

On a spring afternoon near Washington, DC, I witnessed bold and audacious. I got in my car and drove forty miles to a tony private school to watch a basketball tournament, the ESPN Rise National High School Invitational Presented by Gatorade.

Eight of the top boys' basketball teams and four top girls' teams in the country had assembled at the gym of Georgetown Preparatory School. I watched two teams from Maryland with a combined record of 55–5 race up and down the court. In the second game, the featured team represented a high school with ten students, *all* basketball players. Findlay Prep, from Henderson, Nevada, is in many ways a basketball team impersonating a high school. The school was created and bankrolled a few years ago by a Las Vegas car dealer and former University of Nevada-Las Vegas basketball player. Players are recruited from all corners of the country. Basketball season is a perpetual road trip. Other teams in the Rise tournament field had come from Charlotte, North Carolina; New York City; and Mouth of Wilson, Virginia. Findlay could be said to have come from planet Earth.

It was the third annual ESPN Rise National High School

Invitational. Inside the brightly lit gym, it was clear that this event was a showcase for basketball and commerce, though not necessarily in that order.

After the first game, I wandered to the room where reporters waited to interview players and coaches. There was a big painted backdrop with the tournament logo printed on it over and over in wallpaper fashion. A long table was set up with six chairs. In front of each chair sat a bottle of Gatorade, positioned to be visible in every camera shot.

A side door opened and the team from John Carroll High School in Bel Air, Maryland, entered, led by the coach, Tony Martin. His team had just played its thirty-eighth game. Its season had begun in the fall, so long ago that the players could be forgiven for having lost track of which month. Yet this game, Coach Martin said, was different from the rest.

"When you're a kid, what do you dream of?" Martin says. "Jumping on airplanes, getting uniforms, going out to nice dinners, getting gear. [Being in the tournament,] they get a chance to see what it's like in terms of big-time basketball."

The implication of Martin's words was clear: this is what it's like to live in LeBron James's basketball shoes, to play on ESPN, to be treated like stars by a roomful of reporters. We're loving every minute of it. Who wouldn't?

Next to arrive in the interview room was a delegation from Montrose Christian School in Rockville, just up the road. Montrose was favored to win the tournament. This was an easy pick; Montrose was near the top of the Powerade ESPN Rise Fab 50 rankings, which, in addition to serving as an advertising vehicle for the world's most influential sports network and a sports drink company that hydrates the Western World, is a barometer for determining such things.

Coach Stu Vetter was asked if this tournament felt like a national championship to his team. Vetter, perhaps more than any coach in America, craves exactly that. An intense man with singular purpose, Vetter has devoted his life to kids and kids' basketball. He runs his team as if it were in line to be an expansion franchise in the National Basketball Association. One hundred of his former players have gone on to play Division I college basketball. His teams play about ten games each season outside Maryland. As the *Washington Post* has reported, Vetter's staff includes five assistant coaches. "We think we have a pretty great program, almost like a college program," Vetter told the *Post* with evident pride.

"As far as we're concerned," Vetter says in answer to the question, "this is an invitational national championship. This has the feel. It's going to get bigger and bigger as time goes by. Everybody is going to want to get into it. Everyone wants to get into it now. For whatever reasons, state associations or leagues don't want to. The kids do. I don't care what school you're attending. The kids want to play in this tournament."

A few months earlier, I'd visited DeMatha Catholic High School, just a few exits away on the Capital Beltway around DC. I had a conversation with someone there about the ESPN Rise National High School Invitational and got a far different perspective.

DeMatha is a wonderful parochial school, with a legacy of preparing kids to take their place in many facets of society. Coley Mellett, a guitarist with Chuck Mangione, is a DeMatha alumnus. So are Mike Brey, the men's basketball coach at Notre Dame, and Jim Nelson, editor in chief at *GQ*.

Sports are a vital part of the DeMatha experience. Football and basketball teams here are good or great, rarely anything else. The trophy case is longer than the frozen-food aisle at the Kroger's, filled with trophies and plaques celebrating great teams of the past. The true shrine to DeMatha's sports heritage, though, is the old basketball gym. A few years ago, it was renamed the Morgan and Kathy Wootten Gym, in homage to the Stags' former teacher, mentor, and coach and his wife, also a longtime presence at the school. Wootten is revered at DeMatha and is a legend throughout high school basketball. When he retired in 2001, Wootten had amassed more wins than any coach *in the history of basketball.*

At DeMatha, I met with Dan McMahon, the school's principal. McMahon is easy-going and self-effacing. He looks at home in the principal's office, with his wire-rimmed glasses and salt-and-pepper goatee. In conversation, he speaks often of his school's academic mission, yet sports inevitably creeps into the conversation. He is a former youth coach and a confirmed sports buff, but decidedly not a fan of the national invitational that ESPN is running down the road. In fact, McMahon told me he thought the tournament was a flawed idea.

ESPN and its partner, Paragon Marketing Group, have invited DeMatha's boys' team to play in its tournament several times. "We won't participate," McMahon tells me, "even though Paragon Marketing spends a lot of time trying to persuade us we should. It's pretty much the same conversation. They tell us, 'But you'll get to be on TV.' And I tell them, 'I don't care if we're on TV.' We've turned down relentlessly the notion that there should be a national high school basketball championship."

The EPSN Rise National High School Invitational Presented by Gatorade isn't the problem so much as it's a symptom of the problem. In an all-access age, high school sports can be digitized and monetized in ways that were unheard of just a few years ago. ESPN's basketball jamboree, one particularly startling example, airs six tournament games (in HD) on ESPNU (ESPN's station for college and youth sports), three games on ESPN2, and the championship game (won in 2011 by Montrose Christian) on a Saturday at 2 p.m. on the main ESPN network, as big a stage as there is in television sports.

That's not all. Game highlights and interviews are constantly updated on the website ESPNRise. And every dunk, steal, and rebound at the invitational is an opportunity to plug a corporate sponsor ("You're today's Gatorade Top Performer!").

Stu Vetter doesn't mind that high schools such as DeMatha refuse to participate. The National Federation of State High School Associations, the governing body of prep sports, stipulates in its constitution that members may not compete for national championships. Most state athletic associations agree and similarly prevent schools from participating.

Enough is enough, the governing bodies are saying. To play in the ESPN event, some teams have to extend their seasons by a full month. That may serve the interests of adults, like those running the show from the production trucks parked outside the Georgetown Prep gymnasium. Often, it's bad news for kids. As it is, their seasons are an endurance test, stretching, for the top teams, from November through mid-March. That doesn't include preseason workouts, weight-training, summer camps, and tournaments—what amounts to a basketball commitment every week of the year. Findlay Prep played the first game of its 2010–2011 season on November 10. Another month of practice and games simply increases the workload on young players, putting them at greater risk of injury. In a circular way, it even can be argued that a basketball season stretching from the fall to nearly Easter harms schools' overall athletic programs. The basketball stars who would be standouts in track and field, baseball, lacrosse, or any sport for which they suited up are denied that chance. When those spring sports are nearing midseason, they're still reporting to basketball practice.

Clearly, the attention that ESPN and the other national media outlets shower on athletes so young is changing what it means to be a high school athlete. Take the case of Kevin Hart, the high school football player from a small town in Nevada who dreamed of playing for a college power. He'd grown up drinking from the cup of National Signing Day, the first day that high school seniors can sign binding letters of intent for college sports teams. He knew the routine: schedule a news conference and invite the television cameras. In February 2008, Hart did just that, announcing to an eager audience at his high school that he'd accepted a scholarship offer from the University of California-Berkeley. Handshakes, congratulations, and interviews followed. There was a hitch, though. Hart had invented the whole thing. He hadn't been offered a scholarship to play football at Cal. The head coach there had no idea who he was. The only way Kevin Hart was going to a Cal football game, or to any college game, was to buy a ticket.

"I wanted to play D-I [Division I] ball more than anything," Hart said in a statement a few days later. "When I realized that wasn't going to happen, I made up what I wanted to be reality."

A year later, on signing day, one sports media outlet presented a TV investigation into the Hart affair. It was ESPN.

No doubt, the ESPN-ization of high schools has alarmed some, including educators like Dan McMahon of DeMatha, who seem immune to the lure of national TV. But such voices are surprisingly rare. More common is the reaction of the city of Gardner, Kansas, home of the Gardner High

School Trailblazers, a crackerjack football team. In 2010, Gardner's mayor was so pumped that the Trailblazers had been picked for ESPN's schedule that he officially renamed the town "ESPN, Kansas." Fortunately for the residents, it was only for one day.

ESPN's high school basketball invitational commands the same sort of stand-up-and-salute loyalty from some schools. Three that turn up perpetually in the ESPN tournament—Montrose Christian, Findlay Prep, and Oak Hill Academy—don't belong to any state high school sports federations. They're free to roam the country, playing games where they want, when they want, against whomever they please. And they do roam. In a typical season, one of these teams might visit seven states. One year, Findlay Prep's squad reportedly logged thirty thousand miles.

A few years ago, Phil Taylor of *Sports Illustrated* spoke to high school coaches about the corrosive effect that such superteams were having on the high school sports experience. Several shared their fears about powerful corporate interests in school sports, like Nike and ESPN. In Taylor's excellent story, none of the coaches would go public with his concerns. One that dared to be so bold might have had a rough time renewing his school's sneaker sponsorship. Or such was the worry.

"It's good programming for ESPN, but is it good for high school basketball as a whole?" said one coach who spoke to Taylor but asked that his identity be protected. "Are you going to be able to convince your best player to stay and try for a state title when he has a chance to transfer to one of these places where they get on TV and play for the ESPN championship or the Nike championship?"

Is the hyperexposure and adulation good for teen athletes? Best-selling author Buzz Bissinger is convinced it's harmful.

"A good athlete in high school is extolled every day. That's confusing enough for a kid," Bissinger tells me. "Now we tell him he's going to play on national TV and multiply that by a thousand. Do we really expect that kid to care about school?"

Jim Taylor, a sports psychologist and author of *Positive Pushing: How to Raise a Successful and Happy Child,* echoes that concern, noting that a culture of privilege and entitlement grows up around top athletes—TV only exacerbates the situation. Only a fraction of a percent will ever earn a living playing basketball, as impossible as that may seem to students when the ESPN cameras are rolling in their high school gym. But by the time they realize that sobering fact, it's often too late. "They've skated through high school. Then they skate through college until they drop out," says Taylor, who treats high-achieving young athletes in his private practice.

More broadcast exposure is coming. In 2011, ESPN announced a new University of Texas "Longhorn Network," noting that programming would include significant coverage of high school sports around the state. Live-streaming of high school games also is picking up. In 2011, fans in Tennessee, Illinois, Oregon, and elsewhere with an iPhone and 3G connections could watch state championship games on the fledging ESPN3 network.

Rashid Ghazi has a different perspective on the issue of broadcasting teen sports events. Not a lot of sports fans know of Ghazi, but he is indisputably among the most important entrepreneurs in youth sports. Dozens of high school games will be carried on one or another of the ESPN channels sometime in the next twelve months, and, in a large or small way, Ghazi will have had a hand in all of them.

Ghazi is a partner with Paragon Marketing Group. He is a pleasant man with a barely noticeable accent best described as suburban Chicago. He speaks quickly and with something approaching total recall. Throughout our interview, he cites negotiating points from deals conducted ten years ago, then smiles and asks, "Am I giving you more than you need?"

Paragon is a low-profile company whose expertise lies in advising corporations how and where to spend their marketing dollars. Ghazi joined in the 1990s with not many clients and a keen interest in high school sports. In 1998, he dreamt up an idea for a high school basketball game between all-star players from New York and his home city of Chicago. At the time, broadcasts of high school sports on TV was not common, particularly in major media markets. But Ghazi was a believer. He sold the game as a grudge match between the Big Apple and the Windy City, sweet-talked sponsors, and got the game on TV in both markets. The concept was a hit, running for seven years.

In 2002, Ghazi set his sights higher. He convinced ESPN that it ought to telecast a high school basketball game featuring a seventeen-year-old kid from Akron, Ohio, who'd become a national sensation. The player was LeBron James, arguably the most celebrated high school athlete of all time. As a senior, James stood an imposing six foot eight inches tall. On the court, his brilliance as a rebounder and shooter—even as a ball handler—devastated opponents and invited comparisons to the best professional players, heady stuff for a kid still heading off to history and math classes at St. Vincent-St. Mary High School. James didn't do much to discourage those who'd measure him against the best. For the number on his green-and-gold-trimmed uniform, he chose Michael Jordan's familiar twenty-three. Even his birthday—December 30, the same as Tiger Woods— hinted that he belonged with the greats.

James's stellar play lifted his team to the top of the national high school rankings compiled by *USA Today* and ESPN. And if that had slipped your attention, you couldn't help noticing LeBron fever at your local newsstand (in a pre-iPad era, when there were newsstands). In his senior year, James appeared on the covers of both *ESPN the Magazine* and *Sports Illustrated* (the latter of which anointed him "The Chosen One") and got the hero's treatment in *USA Today*, which featured stories on him several times. Television had also discovered James. As a senior, ten of his team's games were beamed across northeast Ohio on a pay-per-view network—with fans charged $7.95 to tune in.

Ghazi was the first to see sponsors and ratings—and lots of dollar signs—in a nationally televised game in which James had a starring role. In 2002, that vision became reality when James led his St. Vincent-St. Mary high school mates against Oak Hill—the same vaunted Oak Hill I would be watching years later in the ESPN national tournament, televised on ESPN2. Ticket brokers offered courtside seats for $100. ESPN sent broadcasters Dick Vitale and Bill Walton, A-list talking heads who typically call college and professional games for the network. Ghazi's confidence that a high school game could draw a sizable TV audience was borne out that night. The game pulled in 1.5 million viewers, the second-largest viewership at the time for anything that ESPN2 had ever shown. "We kind of introduced them to the world of live high school sports," Ghazi says, not in a boastful way.

Ghazi had always considered himself a fan of high school sports. After the LeBron triumph, he could translate that passion into profits. He threw himself into his job, and, in 2005, Paragon and ESPN struck an agreement. ESPN committed to live telecasts of about a dozen football games and a dozen more basketball games featuring schools all over the country. With that partnership, the network entered a new era in its high school coverage. It had traveled a long way from its first live telecast of a high school game—a 1989 matchup between football rivals from Easton, Pennsylvania, and Phillipsburg, New Jersey.

Ghazi's role was that of impresario. He decided which teams made for the most intriguing matchups. Then he traveled the country selling the ideas to high school coaches and principals. Six years after they joined forces, Paragon and ESPN were still in the high school sports business, only much more deeply. Today, ESPN annually airs about fifteen football and fifteen basketball games, from August to February. That is prelude to the high school basketball invitational that ends the first weekend in April. If you miss these games, surf over to ESPN Rise, the website featuring high school team and player rankings, scouting reports, and more.

I asked Ghazi to explain his knack for matchmaking. What elements are key? What distinguishes a game worthy of a national stage on ESPN? Listening to him discuss the matter was like hearing a rock musician ruminate about which song off the next album would be a chart topper. Quickly, he lists a half dozen metrics. One Ghazi favorite is matching teams ranked one and two in an ESPN poll, which, for football, might mean schools from gridiron hotbeds like South Carolina and Florida. Another approach? Selecting teams that feature players lionized in one of a dizzying array of ESPN national player rankings.

Then there are the games that appeal to the stargazer in Ghazi. In 2009, he arranged for Oaks Christian High School in Southern California to fly to Seattle to play Skyline High School—a meeting of West Coast powers. This game had an unusual ratings hook: the Oaks Christian quarterback was Nick Montana, son of NFL Hall of Famer Joe Montana; the Oaks Christian wide receiver was Trey Smith, son of the actors Will Smith and Jada Pinkett; the backup quarterback was Trevor Gretzky, whose father, Wayne, is one of the greats of professional hockey. Still better, a few weeks before the game, Nick Montana announced that he'd attend the University of Washington to play football the next fall—this high school game would be his Puget Sound debut. The only thing missing was a cameo by Kim Kardashian. It was hard to imagine a high school game having greater celebrity stature. "We're not putting a team on just because there's a famous dad—and the son can't play," Ghazi tells me. "Obviously, that wasn't the case here."

As I speak with Ghazi, crowd noise from the Georgetown Prep gym where the opening round of the ESPN high school basketball invitational is underway, rises and falls. Most state high school associations still won't give permission for public schools to participate. Ghazi notes that in its third year, the tournament is wearing down its critics. A year earlier, the North Carolina independent schools changed course and signed up to play, and this year, the New York City Public Schools dropped their objections.

The scene at courtside was a hybrid—a college atmosphere unleashed in a high school gym. ESPN had done some major decorating for the National High School Institute. The midcourt circle had been decorated with the official tournament logo prominently featuring a futuristic expression of the ESPN brand. Nike swooshes were plentiful on the walls and on the players. (I counted five per player on the John Carroll High School squad.) And in case anyone watching at home needed reminding that this was an important tournament—maybe one to be compared to the mega-college-basketball extravaganza played in the same month—ESPN's telecast analyst offered a timely reminder as the game tipped off, blurting into his headset, "It's March Madness time!"

Ghazi has heard the criticisms before both of this tournament and of ESPN's broader high school–sports strategy: It's exploitation. It breeds out-of-control recruiting. It feeds a mindset that sports are more important than excelling at French or AP Chemistry. It turns high school sports into an over-the-top reality show. It's all about the bottom line— Paragon's and ESPN's. I lob these at Ghazi one at a time, expecting he'll lob them back with an edge in his voice. Instead, he responds with patience and tolerance.

"My reaction is, it's a free country," he says. "Everyone can make their choices. They don't have to play." He motions to the logo-laden basketball court. "We don't claim this is a national championship, just a great post-season high school basketball tournament."

Ghazi fills me in about the good things that come out of this tournament: Teams come from all over the country. ESPN picks up the tab for everything—travel, hotel, meals, and a sightseeing excursion. This year, ESPN and Paragon have invited student body presidents—Ghazi was one in high school and college—and editors from high school newspapers of schools that are represented. The kid journalists are at work as we speak—blogging for ESPN Rise.

Ghazi volunteers less about the financial particulars of this tournament and Paragon's other high school ventures. What he says seems at odds with the crowds, excitement, ad panels, and bustling ESPN production crew that buzz around us. These games turn a profit, Ghazi acknowledges, but not a large one. Expenses are high, he explains. Paragon covers all travel costs rung up by high school teams—

players, coaches, the team doctor, and so on. If the South Carolina state champ boards a plane for an ESPN game in Ohio, bills for air travel and hotel rooms land on Ghazi's desk. "Our rule of thumb is, we don't want teams incurring out-of-pocket costs," he tells me.

Revenues from these games also aren't substantial, according to Ghazi. Sponsors willing to pay big bucks to sponsor high school sports are scarce, more so than for college sports and hardly comparable to pro games. Sure, Paragon has agreements with Nike and Gatorade, but the value of those deals is relatively modest. The same goes for the other revenues generated. Paragon collects a small admission fee for the games it brings to ESPN. For a single game, he tells me, ticket prices do not exceed ten dollars. If ten thousand fans turn out for a football game, as sometimes happens, that's $100,000 into the Paragon cash box. But there's a chance that they won't come. "We've gotten into games and lost twenty-five to thirty thousand dollars," Ghazi says.

I was startled to learn how much the schools involved actually earn from their appearances on ESPN. The home team receives a modest fee—$500 to $1,000—which hardly covers the costs incurred hiring security guards to keep order on game day. I asked Ghazi why these games are valuable enough to be plugged into ESPN's gold-plated programming schedule yet pay out so little to the schools in the spotlight.

"The rights fees are nominal because there's not enough money for us to pay astronomical rights fees," Ghazi replies, an answer that seems to be a restatement of my question. "We do thirty games a year. We can't afford to pay two-thousand- or three-thousand-dollar rights fees. It would shut the games down."

Ghazi and I both know that the profits being generated now by Paragon's high school sports franchise are beside the point. The issue is this: having cornered the market on such telecasts, what will they be worth five and ten years down the road? Clearly, Paragon and ESPN believe they're building something with potential to be very lucrative. Worth noting is that they're building it on the backs of sixteen-year-old quarterbacks and point guards.

Ghazi puts it differently: "We've created something we think is unique and original. Are we in business? Absolutely. But this is an investment on our part and ESPN's part."

The criticism by Bissinger and others that Paragon and ESPN are turning up the volume on high school sports in ways that is harmful doesn't impress Ghazi. That the critics include former print journalists—Bissinger and me—strikes him as more than a little ironic.

"Before we came along, newspapers were putting high school sports on the front page for years. No one complained," he says.

Fair point, though most newspapers publicize high school games to readers in whose communities those games take place. Articles have news value. Players being written about are as much newsmakers as the mayor or fire chief. ESPN and Paragon are in the entertainment and event promotion business. They're not covering news so much as creating it. (Some will argue that's not a significant distinction. I maintain that it is.)

Concerns that the ESPN games inflate the importance of sports for high school kids didn't move Ghazi either. "School isn't just about academics," he says. "It's about athletics, too. Just because teams are playing other state champions on TV doesn't mean it's a bad thing."

As I am packing up and thanking Ghazi for his time, he points to my notebook and makes a request. "I'd appreciate it if you'd put this in your book. All you hear about high school these days are the negative things: pregnancy, drop-out rates, how undereducated our kids are compared to the Chinese, gang violence, drugs and alcohol. Negative, negative, negative. That's not what we're doing. Once a week, we're showing the positive, and we're the only organization telling America what's good about high school kids."

I repeat Ghazi's words to Buzz Bissinger, telling him of the various perks for the teams participating in the basketball tournament—the first plane rides that some players have ever taken and sightseeing tours to tourist attractions in Washington, DC.

Bissinger bristles. When he was writing *Friday Night Lights*, the 1990 best seller about a revered and tormented bunch of Texas high school football players, he saw what happens when prep athletes are treated as icons.

"High school is supposed to be based on academics," he says. "So why not go to Washington to be part of a spelling bee? Or to see how the Senate works or to get a tour of the White House? Why are these kids doing it to play in a goddamn insignificant basketball game? It's a bunch of crap. [Paragon and ESPN] are not honest, because they're doing it for money."

Surf over to ESPN Rise, the all-access prep website, click the appropriate tab, and you arrive in the rankings heaven known as the Powerade Fab 50 Super Rankings. ESPN compiles rankings in fifteen high school sports—eight boys' sports, seven girls'—if you count boys' and girls' soccer three times each, one for spring, fall, and winter. On a page spotlighting college recruiting, ESPN offers the ESPNU (the "U" stands for university) 100 (top players, ranked in order, from the current senior class), the super 60 (top junior players), and the terrific 25 (sophomores athletes, ranked and rated, though none is old enough to drive). For each player, a profile page lists information like high school attended, height and weight, and the colleges he or she is considering. It is hard to imagine most high school sophomores giving thought to being high school juniors, much less college students. But these school names come from somewhere.

The number-one-ranked sophomore, Julius Randle, had Kansas, Oklahoma, Ohio State, and Missouri on his list. A thumbnail profile compared his game to that of a star NBA player and gushed, "His touch around the rim and ability to leap multiple times is noteworthy. The young man has counters and power moves. If he likes his matchup, he'll dive right to the blocks and set up shop." Maybe there was a mention of an excellent term paper he turned in or a role he performed admirably in the class play. If so, I couldn't find it.

The compulsion to rate and rank high school teams and athletes is not new. In fact, it's decades old. National Sports News Service, according to ESPNRise.com, had been ranking high school teams since 1944. There were other national polls. But none had impact outside a small circle of high school sports savants and hard-core fans.

Then *USA Today* entered the game. When the "nation's newspaper," as it calls itself, launched in 1982, information presented in the form of charts and polls was central to its strategy. Panned by news junkies, the paper connected with millions of readers, soon becoming one of the most widely read publications in the country.

From the beginning, or nearly so, the sports section featured national rankings of high school sports. With its national reach and readership, it made little sense for *USA Today* to devote space to actual coverage of high school contests. It made a lot of sense, though, to publish a national ranking through which readers could compare teams throughout the country. *USA Today*'s prep rankings—now known as the Super 25—were born.

Over time, *USA Today*'s rankings have expanded to five sports—baseball, softball, football, and boys' and girls' basketball. Exposure for the polls has grown with it. Now the rankings appear in eighty newspapers, including many that, like *USA Today*, are owned by the Gannett Company. They also are featured on about twenty TV stations. Still, the rankings have their largest following on the Web, where *USA Today* maintains a site for every prep sport with final rankings dating back each year to 1997 and links to regional rankings.

I spoke with Monte Lorell, *USA Today*'s longtime sports editor and a much-respected figure within print journalism, about how the rankings are compiled. He parted the curtain slightly, explaining that a staff editor with a deep well of prep knowledge orders the top teams, aided by input from experts around the country. Each sport has a dedicated time slot in the paper and website—football on Tuesdays, boys' basketball on Thursdays, and so on. Clearly, the rankings are popular with readers and a source of revenue for *USA Today*. "You'd be amazed at the traffic" when ranking are posted online, Lorell tells me. "Not NFL level, but there's a spike."

The impact on high school sports, though, is less than desirable.

To reach the top of their leagues or conferences, teams must be talented. To be mentioned in *USA Today*'s Super 25, they must be nearly perfect throughout their seasons. To reach the coveted number-one ranking, a high school squad may have to be outrageous, even headline-grabbing.

As an example, consider the boys' basketball team at Jack Yates Senior High School in Houston, as talented a group of prep shooters and rebounders as there was in America in 2010. Yates High has a proud history—the school is named for a former slave and minister. It has a lauded program in broadcast communications. There is room to improve on the academic front, though. In 2007, a study commissioned by the Associated Press referred to the school as a "dropout factory." At least 40 percent of the entering freshman class failed to reach their senior years.

In basketball, Yates has one of the most gifted teams anywhere. In the 2009–2010 school year, it hardly seemed safe to be in the same gym as Yates. The Lions finished the season 34–0 and swept to the number-one position in the *USA Today* Super 25 Poll. Had there been a Super 25 for sportsmanship, the Lions would have finished out of the top 20,000. Yates didn't just beat opponents; it humiliated many. The team outgunned the opposition by 115, 99 (twice), 98, 90, and 88 points. In an unprecedented show of muscle, on January 6, 2010, Yates demolished rival Lee High School. The final score was 170–35. At halftime, Yates led 100–12.

The game was marred by quick tempers and, in the third quarter, a brawl. When the referees restored order, all but five players on each team had been disqualified.

"I feel very disrespected right now," Lee coach Jacques Armant told the *Houston Chronicle* after the game. "I don't understand why Yates just kept scoring and pressing when they were up so much. These are kids. It isn't good to do that to other young men. . . .

"No coach wants to put his kids in a position to be embarrassed. We have great kids on our team, hard workers, and I am proud that they played the whole game tonight, but you can see how coaches are hesitant to put their kids on the floor with a team that is going to score on them that way."

The Yates coach, Greg Wise, also offered his thoughts.

"We practice running, pressing, trapping every day," he told the *Chronicle*. "If we get to a game and I tell them not to do what we do in practice, I am not coaching well. I am not leaving my starters in the whole game. We have fifteen guys, and all fifteen play.

"We know what people say and some of it is negative, but I believe that Houston is an area that is great for boys' basketball, and I believe we have been on the national stage this year and showed that there is a lot of good basketball here. I think that is good for our team, our community and the Houston area."

For sports psychologist Jim Taylor, Wise's explanation, or "self-justification, defensive tool" in the doctor's words, wasn't persuasive. "Instead of talking about running up the score, it somehow becomes an ethical thing: my kids work so hard and so on," says Taylor. "A game like that exposes everyone involved to unhealthy values, a win-at-all-costs mentality. Unfortunately, it's becoming pervasive in high schools, whether it's cheating on tests or using performance-enhancing drugs," Taylor says.

For all the heat generated by the lopsided game, it seemed to have the desired effect for the Yates team. When the season ended, the Lions were one of three undefeated teams mentioned in the final rankings by *USA Today*. The number-one boys' basketball team in the country was Yates.

I asked *USA Today* sports editor Monte Lorell if he thought a season of mega-blowout victories had helped Yates gain its number-one position. He said he doubted it had been an important factor. "It opens your eyes to how good they are. Outside of that, it probably doesn't have a huge impact," he told me.

I couldn't reach Coach Wise to ask the same question. I wonder if he would have agreed.

SIX

Selling Hope

It was not a typical workday for me. Let's begin there. I was dressed more casually than is normal—which takes effort. My usual attire consists of sneakers, jeans, and a wrinkled shirt. This day, I went to work wearing my perspiration-wicking Baltimore Pacemakers T-shirt, running shorts, running cap (turned backward), and running shoes.

The biggest departure from the everyday, though, was the object that I held in my hands. Not a pen, a reporter's notebook, or even an iPhone. On a misty morning in March, I was cradling a compact ball, multicolored and deceptively heavy. It looked like a small watermelon and felt like it had a couple of rocks inside.

I was being indoctrinated into SPARQ—Speed, Power, Agility, Reaction, and Quickness—a physical literacy test taken by tens of thousands of high school athletes each year. If you burn with ambition to play sports in college, a SPARQ test and a SPARQ rating are worth going out of your way for. At least so says Nike, which has a marketing relationship with SPARQ. For many reasons, I wasn't the usual SPARQ contestant. I'm bald, wrinkled, and I go to sleep early—9:15 p.m. being something of a mandatory bedtime. At the time of taking the SPARQ test, I was fifty-four, older than most of the college coaches the usual SPARQ test-takers are trying to impress. I was mildly curious about my fitness and how it might compare to that of kids in their athletic primes. In that sense, I did have something in common with the target demographic. Anyway, here I was, about to submit to four tests comprising SPARQ's football evaluation.

Test number one, the kneeling powerball toss. This is odd. I'm in the backyard of Patrick Marsh, a local SPARQ trainer (to proctor the test, trainers must be "certified" by Nike), with a 4.4-pound medicine ball cradled in my hands. Per instructions from Pat, I'm on my knees facing an expanse of green lawn.

On the first throw, I rock, groan, and eventually throw. Then I lurch forward and fall on my face. After each subsequent attempt, Marsh snaps a tape measure to the spot on the grass where the ball has fallen and jots notes on his clipboard. Then he totals my score and shares the news. Fighting a smile, he tells me that I've placed in the *first* percentile. In a field of tens of thousands of kids SPARQ-tested each year, I am last.

Nike's SPARQ is the tip of the iceberg. The business of sports tryouts is booming. In recent years, dozens of companies have leaped in ranging from the corporate giants to small operators in Anytown, USA. The market they are tapping, though, is largely the same—high school players focused on the dream of becoming college athletes. And if an athletic scholarship is part of the deal, all the better.

For these young athletes, the challenge is to sell themselves to college coaches. Doing so means trying to stand out in a crowd of thousands if not tens of thousands of other high school athletes. The companies and entrepreneurs involved provide a boost, or claim they do. The precise services differ by sport. For lacrosse and field hockey hopefuls, the way to be seen is to participate in offseason tournaments that serve as organized tryouts. The important ones are attended by dozens of college coaches, who supposedly can evaluate hundreds of players in a weekend. In baseball, players pay hundreds of dollars and sometimes more to participate in showcases. Five hundred young athletes might show up because they hope to impress the few dozen coaches who are attending. In these and other sports, college coaches often operate summer sports camps. Many of the kids who attend do so because they believe they're gaining valuable face time with a coach they hope to one day play for. So their parents pay the camp registration fee.

In football, college coaches operate under restraints that stop them from scouting players as coaches in other sports do. As a result, a wide range of services has grown up around grading high school football talent and serve as the coaches' eyes and ears. Some of these companies charge exorbitant fees. Others charge nothing—their businesses rely on selling related stuff. In most cases, it's not clear that they deliver what they say they do—or what we hope they will.

The problem is simple: there are far more kids hoping to play college sports than roster spots for them. The math is quite discouraging. And it hasn't gotten better since 2009, when I reported on it in my book *Until It Hurts*. According to the National Collegiate Athletic Association, fewer than seven high school players in a hundred move from prep to college teams. That includes just 5.7 percent of boys' soccer players, 3.1 percent of women's basketball players, and 2.9 percent of men's basketball players. Football isn't much better—just 5.8 percent of those off high school rosters end up playing in college.

The idea that sports will pay for college is also a myth for all but a few. The average athletic scholarship for the 138,216 athletes in Division I or Division II schools in 2003–04 was $10,409, about half the cost of attending state universities and a fifth the tuition at their private counterparts. As I noted in *Until It Hurts,* the best-compensated college athletes are the ones playing ice hockey. Both men and women players brought home, on average, 80 percent of full scholarships, or slightly more than $20,000 per player. On the low end of the scale are scholarships for sports such as volleyball, soccer, and, for men, wrestling. For their efforts, wrestlers who had earned athletic scholarships picked up just 37 percent of total tuition, a little more than $6,700, according to a 2008 *New York Times* report.

If more parents knew these statistics, and took them to heart, perhaps none of them would pay for their children to try out for a college coach. Instead, though, this industry is growing like a wild mushroom. And some of the companies that are jumping in are making some amazing claims.

Case in point: National Underclassmen Combines, a high-profile and sometimes self-congratulatory entry into the football-tryout business. The company is testament to the hard work and vision of its founder, David Schuman.

Schuman's story attests to the wide-open nature of this booming niche. In 2005, he tacked up a few flyers in local high schools about a football combine he would be staging. The response was heartening—about 140 kids showed up. Now Schuman presides over a combine empire. There seem to be few places yet visited by National Underclassmen. In 2011, the company ran combines in Phoenix, Las Vegas, Houston, Savannah, Fort Lauderdale, Albuquerque, Los Angeles, Baton Rouge, Tallahassee, and Pensacola—all in February. There are NUC combines not only for high school juniors but also for tenth graders, ninth graders, and, yes, eighth graders. In addition to the company's standard football tryouts, there is the All-World Strongman Challenge, the All-World Youth Combine, and the All-World Seniors Challenge.

Clearly, Schuman is running a growing business. In 2011, NUC issued a press release to announce the company's "expansion into new cities" and to share the news that the year before 24,000 kids had "participated" in NUC-sponsored events. More notable was a statistic offered about the company's success in helping youth players play college ball. "At the NUC," Schuman says, "our goal has been to help high school football athletes—in particular Freshman and Sophomores, but we have expanded to Juniors and 8th graders to help them gain early exposure to colleges to showcase their skills." And it continues: "20% of our athletes have gone on to receive scholarships and over 70% have gone on to play college football."

Those percentages are impressive. They also raise eyebrows. According to the National Collegiate Athletic Association, about 1.1 million young athletes (mostly boys, but not all) are members of high school football teams. Nearly 317,000 are seniors. Just 6 percent of high school football players will be playing in college the following fall.

If 70 percent of NUC youth football customers are playing in college, and if all are playing for NCAA member schools—the Main Street of collegiate sports and the ambition of most—then one in four college players has crossed paths with NUC, an astonishing success rate. (There are collegiate alternatives affiliated with the lesser-known NAIA, or National Association of Intercollegiate Athletics, and with two-year junior colleges; perhaps NUC includes these.)

NUC must have an office filled with employees tasked only with tracking the whereabouts of its teen alumni. Imagine the intelligence gathering required to substantiate that more than ten thousand people are on or off college football rosters. How do they do it? And are such claims audited?

I e-mailed David Schuman, explaining the book I was writing and my curiosity about his stats. Where had they come from? "I'd be interested in speaking with you about that and having a look at the research that supports it," I wrote.

I did get an e-mail back—an automated one—thanking me for my inquiry and letting me know that I'd be hearing back as soon as possible. Despite other attempts to reach him, I never did.

Whether NUC's claims are to be believed isn't the primary issue—whether kids benefits from the services it offers is. Still, the company's remarkable statistics do invite skepticism. "I have no time for these kinds of people," one sports training source replied when we spoke about the 70 percent figure. "In the Old West they would have been selling snake oil."

What's startling about the recruiting industry is the antipathy of many high school coaches toward it.

"I am not a fan and I want to throw up at the money some people are making off these things," John Sanders, the football coach at Saguaro High School in Scottsdale, Arizona, told the *East Valley Tribune*—a common reaction. "Every coach is different. I think getting these kids to college is my job. Not everyone has that same belief. I can help my players get to all levels of college from D-I to NAIA."

A veteran lacrosse coach sought me out to speak about the phenomenon of summer camps run by college coaches, a particular irritation for him. He explained how this had all evolved over the past two decades or so, to the point where parents and kids believe they have little choice but to travel to campuses and pay camp tuition to be more than a blip on the coaches' recruiting radar. It's not uncommon for kids and parents to zigzag the country for weeks, hitting three or four camps and spending thousands of dollars on flights and hotels.

"Ninety percent of the kids have it in their mind [that] they'll end up playing for that school and that coach—the parents believe too," says the coach, who asked not to be named. "Out of the hundreds who show up, how many is the coach really interested in? Six or seven?"

Meanwhile, such camps generate sizable sums. One coach at a women's college lacrosse powerhouse typically holds six camps per summer. Each camp fills up to four hundred campers, and each camper pays a registration fee of $450. There are operating expenses for the camp promoters, of course, for everything from paying the college players who serve as counselors, providing meals and dormitory rooms. Still, a successful college coach in lacrosse, football or soccer—any sport in which scholarships are up for grabs and families are aggressively seeking one—can turn a tidy profit.

In *Until It Hurts*, I wrote at length about my misadventures guiding the baseball life of my son Ben, including my spare-no-expense approach to the college recruiting game. Ben was a good player in high school, attaining All-Conference honors as a pitcher and middle-of-the-order power hitter. He wanted to play baseball in college. And I convinced myself that this was an entirely reasonable goal, despite ample evidence that it was not. (One example: My son's summer-league coach, a wise and blunt man, explaining to me, "Your son will *not* play baseball in college.")

Still, I forged ahead, agreeing to send Ben to a fall weekend camp at a top academic school he had an interest in.

This was a dad's dream, because the school also was my alma mater; I was watching my kid playing baseball on my old campus, in front of the head baseball coach for my beloved team. Within a matter of hours, I felt as if I'd watched several hundred dollars fall out of my pocket and the coach pick it up. There were 150 players, maybe more, in camp. There were seven or eight catchers—including Ben—vying for workout time.

SPARQ is a credential for athletes, a resource for college coaches. Or so goes the marketing pitch. Its vast database of high school players is also fun to play with and as addictive as Facebook. When I typed "Manning" into the search engine, nothing came back on the NFL star brothers, Peyton and Eli. But I did learn about twelve other Mannings across the country who'd been SPARQ-rated, among them Donaldven, Travis, Lenzell, and Jalen. For no particular reason, I checked the SPARQ ratings of my direct competition—other players sharing my last name. I found three—Kevin and Kareem from Somerset, New Jersey, and Aries from Tucson.

Most combines charge for signing up—$75 to $150 being a typical registration fee. Nike tryouts are free, as is the swag passed out at each combine—form-fitting short-sleeve T-shirts and backpacks slathered in Swooshes. This has several effects, all no doubt calculated by Nike. First, attendance tends to be huge. A thousand or more kids might show up at a Nike camp, two or three times the attendance at one of its pay-to-play competitors. Second, Nike's policy tends to build brand loyalty. High school kids, with their swagger and free-spending habits, are a prime demographic for the Nike brand. SPARQ serves as a loss leader of sorts, entertainment for customers who will be buying swoosh gear for years to come.

There is a short-term return for the company too. Surrounding the free experience is a lot that is not free, such as those atomic-green medicine balls ($35), the SPARQ speed ladder ($40), and weighted "resist" Vest ($175) . There's also training for the test. Nike can provide a boost here too. Parents can choose from a group of SPARQ-certified trainers around the country who will work with players on the skills measured by the combines—for a fee, of course.

Whether college coaches pay attention to SPARQ is difficult to say. One of SPARQ's most ardent supporters is Andy Bark, a giant among youth sports entrepreneurs. In the 1980s, when few saw the business possibilities in high school–sports media, Bark was creating an empire with a company he called Student Sports. Later, he entered the high school–recruiting business and was in on the founding of SPARQ. These days, Bark works for ESPN and has no role in SPARQ. Still, it's hardly a surprise to hear him praise the testing methodology. "Is it part of the equation? Sure," Bark says when asked if college coaches consider SPARQ ratings. This is verifiable, he tells me. Just go online and watch the frenzied attention received by elite players after posting a really fast time in, say, the 40-yard dash. "You'll see players who had no offers have twenty offers within two or three days," he says.

College coaches also praise SPARQ, particularly those with marketing ties to Nike and, by extension, to SPARQ. That is, many coaches. Of 120 colleges and universities competing in the Football Bowl Division, the heavyweight class of collegiate football, more than half speak at Nike-sponsored events or have sponsorship deals with the sports apparel and footwear giant. They owe a lot to Nike, perhaps including loyalty. Occasionally, there are unguarded moments, and a coach's true feelings or lack of feeling about SPARQ will peek through.

In 2008, Pete Carroll, then coach of the University of Southern California football team, was being interviewed for a video intended for Nike's website. According to the *Oregonian* newspaper, the interview went as follows:

INTERVIEWER: And how important is Nike SPARQ Training to your upcoming team this year?

CARROLL (looking off camera): Um, lemme ask you a question here. I don't know what Nike SPARQ [training is].

The further removed that sports training experts are from the force field of Nike, National Underclassmen, and other companies, the more skeptical they seem about the services they offer.

Vern Gambetta is as experienced and reputable a sports trainer as you will find working today. His credentials are too many to mention here but include having served as a trainer for Major League Baseball and professional soccer teams, and as personal conditioning coach to Monica Seles, the former women's tennis star. Gambetta has been working with high school kids for years and has a keen eye for which ones have a shot to make it at the college level. When I asked him how many kids paying good money or traveling great distances to attend football combines truly have a shot to play college football one day, he thinks for a moment. The figure he gives me falls slightly short of the 70 percent given in the National Underclassmen Combines press release.

"I'll go high and say fifteen percent," he says. Which means 85 percent have no chance whatsoever. Still, those kids and their disposable income are critical to the entire college-recruiting enterprise. Promoters need the also-ran high school kids to show up at their event as much as they do the stud athletes—probably more.

"If they had to rely on high school kids who are really qualified for the few number of scholarships, there would be no [combine] business," Gambetta says. "That's all it comes down to: there would be no business."

These odds seem to be discouragement to few families. In 2010, Nike reported that more than fifteen thousand high school players were "tested and rated." A year later, Nike staged SPARQ combines from January to June in sixteen cities, from Hawaii to Alabama.

A SPARQ combine held in Baltimore in 2011 was fairly typical—1,300 teenaged players from Maryland, Pennsylvania, New Jersey, New York, Virginia, and elsewhere, converging on the football stadium at Coppin State University. In their shorts and Nike T-shirts (free to all the players who attend), they looked like they were about to choose up sides for the world's largest touch-football game. But soon the young players stepped into the long lines that snaked around the turf field, waiting for their turns to sprint, throw, and grunt. Meanwhile, in the grandstand, fathers and mothers, sisters and brothers, watched the scene unfold. Some sipped coffee and read newspapers, hiding their anxiety or trying to. Others were on their feet for hours on end, seeming to take in everything that happened on the turf field and in something of a trance when their player of interest finally made it to the front of the line.

At times, football felt like a footnote. The main event seemed to be on the edges of the field where an unlikely bazaar was underway. Banners and signs fluttered everywhere—ESPN Rise, Nike, SPARQ, even the U.S. Army. As players sipped free Gatorade, Army recruiters in fatigues engaged them, schmoozing and offering a velvet-glove re-

cruiting pitch. Next door, Xenith, a high-tech helmet manufacturer, showed off the latest in protective head gear. And
as the high school players filed off the field, many lingered
at seemingly the most popular hangout in the stadium that
morning, the Nike merchandise zone. As speakers blared
rap songs, players stopped to shop and look over manne-
quins dressed in the latest Nike uniforms of the University
of Florida, Virginia Tech, and Boise State.

The scene was old hat to Christopher Shaw, a 148-pound
running back who was attending his third SPARQ combine.
This one was a relatively short trip from his home in Pennsylvania. Earlier, he'd caught up with the SPARQ tour in
Pittsburgh and Salt Lake City. Despite his slender build, he
had his sights set on playing for Bethune-Cookman, a his-
torically black college with a rich football heritage. He was
in Baltimore, he explains, "to see where I'm at performance-
wise." And because, like the other kids assembled here, he
thought it was a pretty cool place to be. "I like the fact Nike
is a part of this."

Many players had burned a tank of gas to get to Baltimore.
Lucas Smissen, a lean wide receiver and high school junior,
was in town from Lynchburg, Virginia. His hope was to run
so fast that the coaches at Liberty University in his hometown would have no choice but to pay attention. Randall
Anderson, a defensive end who at six-foot four towered over
other players, had cruised in from New Castle, Delaware.
Ebenezer Ogundeko, an enormous player who reported his
height at six-foot three, came with three teammates from
Brooklyn. "I'd planned to come here since January."

Eamon Van-Callahan, a junior from Severna Park, Maryland, seemed to speak for many when he surveyed the scene
and said, "I think it's pretty crazy. I knew it was a big deal,
but I didn't know it was a 'huge-line, hundred-kids-on-the-
field' big deal."

Nike is hardly alone in seeking profit in college recruiting. A recent competitor is Under Armour, also a giant in selling athletic apparel and gear. In 2009, Under Armour announced it was going into the combine business with another major sports brand, IMG. The partnership made sense. IMG is one of the world's great sports promoters. It has cut endorsement deals for Tiger Woods and negotiates TV agreements for Wimbledon tennis matches. It operates the IMG Academies, a 180-acre, posh campus, about thirty miles south of Tampa, where thousands of kids train in tennis, golf, soccer, baseball, hockey, and other sports.

Under Armour's entry into the business was timed to blunt Nike's introduction of a SPARQ cross-training shoe—Under Armour introduced its own cross trainer. The company, led by charismatic founder Kevin Plank, had a larger plan. It borrowed heavily from the Nike playbook, coming up with a clever name for its college sports combine—Combine360. Then it took the show on the road, scheduling the tryouts in cities around the country.

In an important respect, Under Armour and Nike go in different directions. Unlike Nike's freebie model, Under Armour's combines collect a registration fee that can range up to about $300. Plank does not apologize for that. Rather, he turns it to his company's advantage—or tries to. "This isn't about showing up and giving them a six-dollar cotton T-shirt," he told the *Sports Business Journal.*

Under Armour combines have a more exclusive feel. There are attendance limits. Sometimes they sell out. One football player at the Baltimore SPARQ combine expressed surprise at the turnout. At an Under Armour event, the cutoff was about three hundred. "This is way less exclusive."

J.C. Pinkney, the football coach at Frederick Douglass High School in Upper Marlboro, Maryland, also spoke well of Nike. Kids at his school in a hard-scrabble neighborhood get little in the way of new equipment and manicured fields. Every year, they do get a chance to run the 40 at a SPARQ event in the area. Pinkney well understands that for Nike the endgame is moving merchandise. Still, he says, "They're a multibillion dollar company, but they did that for free, which I respect."

Competition among companies offering college auditions seems to stiffen each year. Next Level Nation, based in Jessup, Maryland, targets children in the sixth grade. At the All- State Middle School Combine, the company says it is on the lookout for "the next cream of the crop of talent." Entry fee: $50.

How are such services changing youth sports? In ways we have overlooked, do they put kids at risk? Do they, for example, encourage, even glamorize, year-round specialization?

Each year, it is more difficult to resist the continuous loop of games, camps, tournaments, combines, and so on— partly because each year there are more that seem vital to take part in. A coach who has been associated with a girls' lacrosse program for many years expressed his concern to me about this issue. He had just completed a stretch of six weeks in which his team had played in five tournaments— all far enough from home that parents and players had to spend a night or more in a hotel. The girls were exhausted; the coaches (according to him) ambivalent about the money spent and the experience gained. Yet some parents supported the schedule—they feared that anything less and their children might miss out on something.

"On the one hand, they see that it's too much, that their kids are worn out, tired of traveling, and tired even of lacrosse, which they love," this coach tells me. "On the other, they can't take a chance [on missing an opportunity]."

• • •

The same psychology explains the rise of college recruiting enterprise on the Web. If you can a find a wife at eHarmony, buy loafers at Zappos, and order dessert at Ice Cream Cake Online, why not a college scholarship at beRecruited.com?

A dozen or more college recruiting consultants operate in cyberspace. Just the names suggest they are scholarship pipelines—in addition to beRecruited.com, there are PrepChamps.com, Recruit-Me.com, ShowcaseU.com, and others.

Each of these companies makes impressive claims. BeRecruited.com calls itself "the largest and most successful online network connecting high school athletes and college coaches." A news crawl at the site offers continuous updates on athletes who have landed lucrative scholarships with the assistance of the company. SportsWorx.com tells us it's "your ticket to college." Recruit-Me pledges to share "THE SECRETS of getting recruited." Collegiate Sports of America may be the brashest of all. The Woodland Hills, California–based company says it stands ready to tap into a network of "over 32,000 registered college coaches."

The companies offer a range of services. For example, Collegiate Sports of America stages combines in softball with prices ranging up to $700. Some companies provide hands-on consulting, while others follow the do-it-yourself model—post your own video and load your profile. Virtually all suggest that they have clout with college coaches or a long record of matching students with schools.

Testing the accuracy of claims like that can be hard to do. On the beRecruited site, I followed a news ticker for a few minutes and collected the names of a few players listed as having recently linked up with college programs. There was no assertion that beRecruited had closed these deals, but any child or parent visiting the site might assume as much. One of the athletes listed was a volleyball player named Abby who, the site said, had just signed to play at Grand Valley State, a Division II university in Allendale, Michigan.

I was curious whether beRecruited deserved credit for Abby's success. I located her school and then her father, a high school football and volleyball coach. He confirmed that his daughter had registered at beRecruited—she hadn't paid anything for the service—and was quite satisfied. Abby, it turned out, wasn't referred by the service to a single college coach. Nor had her dad any reason to believe that any coach had logged onto the site and viewed her profile. Rather, Abby used the beRecruited site to collect the names and addresses of college coaches on file there. Armed with this widely available, public information, she sent off personal letters and e-mails.

"A lot of kids have no idea how to get a hold of coaches. It was a good resource for that, at least," Abby's father told me.

A recent *Wall Street Journal* article cited several success stories involving the services. The most impressive was about tiny Jamestown College, in North Dakota. The *Journal* reported that nine freshmen—from Arizona, Texas, and South Carolina—were on the roster of the football team at the liberal arts school with an enrollment of about 1,100 students: "The coach found them on beRecruited.com and offered them scholarships."

Coaches at larger schools are less likely to rely on recruiting services—or be aware they exist. I called a few, and the most favorable response I heard was, "Well, it's not a total rip-off."

"I don't look at the individuals running these businesses as taking advantage of parents," says Mike Zandler, assistant baseball coach and recruiting coordinator at Davidson College in North Carolina, a respected Division I school. He'd never heard of half of many of the dot-com experts I mentioned. "From our perspective, it's not necessary," he tells me. "I want to deal with the player himself."

I had nearly the same conversation with Tara Vanderveer, coach of Stanford's national champion women's basketball team. "If I get an e-mail from a person—a young player or a parent—I respond to it. I do not respond to 'be recruited or the websites that tell me about people. I just delete them," she says.

A personal letter or e-mail tells Vanderveer something important: that she is dealing with someone with the confidence and skills to communicate directly. That doesn't substitute for a feathery jump shot, but she says it gets her attention. "The key for me is a lot of personal communication. Hearing from the player, 'I'm playing at this event,' 'Here are my grades.' If I had any advice for athletes about college recruiting, it would be do the work yourself."

I asked Ricky Fried, women's lacrosse coach at Georgetown, whether he could recall offering a scholarship or even just a place on the team to a player who'd contacted him through a scouting service or website. "If there is a player who worked through a recruiting service, our interest in that player would not have been for that reason," he said. "I can tell you that emphatically."

I asked these coaches about player videos. Whether they use recruiting websites or go it alone, many high school players upgrade their pitch with video. Typically, these productions run four or five minutes and show the player performing skills that can be evaluated by the coaches without having to see the player in person. A baseball catcher might be shown blocking balls in the dirt. A volleyball player leaping at the net and spiking. And so on.

Coaches receive thousands of these videos. So parents feel a responsibility to produce one that stands out. Over the years, the videos have turned into Darryl Zanuck productions, complete with theme music, plot lines, and, at the end, credits. One Connecticut-based firm charges $250 for the "basic package"—a testimonial running four to six minutes. Or opt for the long-form movie (seven to nine minutes) for $350. Watching the recruiting video of one highly skilled field hockey player, I felt momentary sympathy for the player's high school coach who appears on screen to offer a glowing, if somewhat coded, tribute: "She excels at jab tackles. She times them very well." Does the coach have to compose a different glowing tribute for each kid's video?

Mike Zandler, the Davidson baseball assistant coach, discouraged parents from going overboard. He notes that in a given year his program hears from more than a thousand prospects. The entire baseball team has four baseball scholarships to offer. Sometimes those are divided into partial scholarships, eight half scholarships, or even smaller slices. Other years, one full scholarship might go to a star. Videos—even those with impeccable cinematography—do not play a role, he said.

"It's comical, some of the videos we receive. It's obvious that the players have spent hundreds if not thousands of dollars," Zandler tells me. "A few years ago, we received one—great graphics, four or five teacher and coach interviews discussing the player's character and work ethic. It was so put together that I started referring to the player as 'The Video.'"

Ricky Fried has his own story about players and parents trying too hard to impress. "It sounds silly," Fried says, "but one thing you can evaluate is the parents. Some are recording videos which they post to YouTube. They forget that the volume is on and that we're hearing everything they say. I've never [heard] anything egregious. You do get a sense whether this is a parent enjoying their kids or living through them."

Regrettably, if not surprisingly, my SPARQ tryout didn't lead to a college scholarship. I turned out to be ungifted in all four football drills—kneeling powerball throw, shuttle run, 40-yard dash, and vertical jump.

The shuttle run—run five yards this way, ten that way, five this way—was my best event. I zoomed in with a time of 5.72 seconds, placing me with the bottom four percent of all test-takers. In the other three events, I was at rock bottom, not surprising given my advanced age.

The whole test lasted forty minutes. Time enough for trainer Patrick Marsh to assess my showing and offer a positive spin. "In the shuttle run, your wisdom and experience showed," he said looking up from his clipboard. It was one of those statements that isn't true but is appreciated anyway. I left his home feeling that, in spite of everything, I was a typical SPARQ customer. There was no chance I'd ever play college sports, and I was more interested than ever in buying Nike gear.

SEVEN

Making Progress, and Maybe a Fortune

Brendan Sullivan's resume is one of the more intriguing I've encountered in youth sports. It's difficult to capture Sullivan's background in a few sentences. He's a Stanford grad, a former collegiate and minor league baseball player, the son of one of the most famous criminal defense attorneys in America—and a Georgetown Law School dropout. His business card doesn't list any of that though. It identifies Sullivan as founder and president of Headfirst, a Washington, DC–based summer camp and baseball instruction company.

Sullivan's business covers a wide swath of the youth-sports economy. During summers, Headfirst stages day camps for kids ranging from kindergarteners to twelve-year-olds. There are the typical camp sports—baseball, lacrosse, and soccer—and non-sports options too, like "mad science"—"a week of fun with amazing robots"—and even a $410 per week cooking session for little ones.

The other side of Sullivan's sports operation is hardly kid stuff. Through two companies, Honor Roll Camps and Diamond College Advisory Team, the former pro-baseball player markets the college-sports dream to more than a thousand teenagers each year. Sullivan's model is different from that of most college audition and tryout-mill companies. His focus is on kids hoping to play baseball at elite, academically rigorous schools like Stanford (his alma mater), Duke, or in the Ivy League. What Sullivan sells isn't for everyone, and it certainly isn't cheap. Diamond College Advisory Team's fee for guiding teenagers through college recruiting— meetings with counselors and skill assessments—runs as much as $5,695.

That's what Sullivan's company has become, but it's miles from what it was when he started more than a decade ago. In 1996, Sullivan was pitching late in the season for the Idaho Falls Braves, a minor league team in a small town, and thinking about what he'd do over the winter back in DC. He pulled one of his minor-league baseball cards from his pocket and decided to turn it into a business. "I can assure you there were no Kinko's in Idaho Falls at that point. I found a copy shop, Xeroxed my baseball card, and put a few bullet points on it," he says. Then he paged through the student directory of a local private school and started taking down addresses. "I mailed it to everyone in the seventh grade and under, offering pitching lessons."

Sullivan had stumbled into his future. Parents liked him, and a friend, a former high school classmate, Rob Elwood, joined him in the fledging business. The players enjoyed their visits with him and improved their form. Sullivan also talked about the value of hard work, doing your best, and being a good teammate. The parents appreciated the influence he was having on their kids. "We were good coaches," he tells me. "I think more importantly we were the type of coaches that parents in this area wanted their kids to be around. We were academic-minded. Running through every program were the ideas of leadership, character development, and hustle. Clichés, in a way, but [they were] all the things that aren't focused on enough for kids at that age in sports."

The business grew. When Sullivan's pitching career ended several years later, he decided he could turn the sideline into a full-time business. With his ex-teammate, he launched Headfirst and quickly became the proprietor of a company popular among kids who loved baseball and among parents who could afford the personal instruction.

Sullivan's college-tryout business seems far removed from those early days. Sullivan tries to convince me it isn't. As he tells it, he's still trying to help kids be the players they can be. He tells me about a young man named Matt, "one of my favorite kids we've ever had. I've known him since he was little. I gave him and his buddies a pitching lesson at Friendship Playground back in the very early days of Headfirst."

A few years ago, Matt signed up for a Headfirst college-tryout camp. He attracted quite a bit of interest among coaches from Ivy League schools, Sullivan tells me, and eventually accepted an offer to attend Princeton. In his first at bat of his freshman season, Matt hit a home run.

"Those are special things. They mean as much to you as anything that happens," Sullivan tells me.

Sullivan's business caters to the wealthy and ambitious in DC and around the country. There are few inner-city kids from single-parent families attending Headfirst showcases. For children from such backgrounds, there are often too many hurdles. Suburban kids have been playing baseball for years on rec teams and travel teams. Some have enjoyed the additional experience and exposure of private lessons and out-of-town tournaments. Such experiences are beyond the reach of many city kids. In fact, relatively few city kids play baseball anymore, as I was reminded recently when speaking with the coach of an inner-city high school team in Baltimore.

The coach, an enthusiastic guy and, from what I'd heard, a dedicated mentor to his players, told me that twenty-eight young ballplayers had tried out for the team earlier that spring. Just eleven had ever played organized baseball. It is doubtful that there is a suburban school in the country with a percentage so low. For city kids who do play baseball at a high level, money is likely to be an issue. It takes thousands, sometimes tens of thousands of dollars, to participate in college recruiting. Kids living in one-bedroom apartments typically don't have it. Sullivan didn't create the economic chasm, and he does what he can to reach out to kids from disadvantaged backgrounds. But there's no doubt that, more than ever, in youth sports money talks.

In fact, money pushes and pulls Sullivan's business from all sides. For many years, Sullivan has served the dozens of college coaches who stop in at his camps to have a look at the next crop of high school talent. They still do, but lately some of these coaches are also his competitors. Seeing the big bucks that Sullivan and promoters like him make, coaches have started their own tryout camps in baseball, lacrosse, and other sports. They wear many hats: that of promoter, talent judge, and cashier. One year, the coaches were attending Sullivan's camps. The next, he claims, they were mailing out flyers to high school kids inviting them to their camps and advising them to skip Sullivan's.

Sullivan won't speak publicly about them or their alleged tactics. But he admits that he's in a business—the business of helping kids get recruited to play college sports—in which you've got to watch your back. "There's a huge market right now," Sullivan says. "Everybody wants to put their hands in it in some way."

• • •

Jess Heald's career in the business of youth sports is a study in happenstance. Almost nothing turned out as planned. Fifty years later, he is one of the most important people to have worked in the industry.

Heald didn't expect to spend his life engineering sports equipment. He was an aerospace engineer whose training prepared him to seek efficiencies in airplane design. And he certainly didn't foresee becoming one of the founding fathers of a product that delivers tens of millions of dollars in profits for sporting goods companies every year—metal baseball bats. But that happened too.

Heald would want this to be clear at the start: he didn't invent the aluminum baseball bat. That distinction goes to a Pittsburgh man, Anthony Merola, who turned out to be far better at developing the concept than in building something that functioned acceptably. In the late 1960s, Merola spent several years fiddling with a design before he introduced an aluminum softball bat that looked and swung like a pool cue. It flopped.

Then Heald came along. He'd was living in Tullahoma, Tennessee, and working in aerospace. At the Boy Scouts meetings he attended with his son, Heald kept running into the father of another boy, the owner of Worth Sports, a local sporting-goods company. John Parrish Sr. had plans to expand his business into the production of wood baseball bats.

When Heald spoke with him, Parrish had just come back from a meeting where he'd learned of a competing company experimenting with bats from aluminum tubing. As Heald recalls, Parrish told him, "We're about to go into the wood bat business. If this thing takes off, it could have a very bad effect on us."

Parrish asked his friend to look into the physics of bat-making and work up a plan for building bats from aluminum. Heald concluded that "not only did it make sense. But you could make one a helluva lot better than the pool-cue manufacturer was doing."

Heald joined Worth in 1970, the year before it became the first major company to hit the market with bats made out of aluminum. A year after, the company introduced the first official Little League aluminum bat. In 1972, Worth was first with aluminum bats for college teams. It was years before competitors like Easton and Louisville Slugger caught up.

Heald told me this story from Taos, New Mexico, where he lives in retirement. We spoke about the bat brain trust. What had Worth been thinking in those days? What gave Parrish and the others at the company confidence that, after a century of embracing wood, kids and parents would run into stores and plunk down good money for aluminum?

What Heald told me came as a surprise.

From the start, the bat executives were banking on cost. Then, as now, metal bats cost more than comparable wood models—in the early years, eight to ten dollars for metal compared to five for wood. Still, metal bats were seen as money savers in part because they were largely indestructible. In the old days, a youth league might have to commit half its budget to stocking and restocking wood bats. They'd break, splinter, and crack at an alarming rate, so quickly that an average youth team might need to replenish its stock completely during a season. Not so with metal. "One aluminum bat would outlast seven [wood models]," Heald tells me. In the long run, the savings were huge. Leagues quickly caught on that metal bats were a stunning cost saver.

Metal bats opened the sport to younger players. Before

these bats arrived, baseball began at age eight for most kids and sometimes nine. Little ones lacked the strength to lift, much less swing, heavier wood bats. The sport was largely beyond their reach.

"When I was growing up," Heald says, "the question always asked about a young kid was: 'Is he old enough to swing the bat?' I remember that so clearly. Because in the wood-bat era, some kids weren't. Now you would never hear that question."

Heald credits metal bats for adding millions of new ballplayers, all needing new mitts, caps, shoes, and, of course, bats. Tee Ball had been around since the late 1950s. It became commonplace in the 1970 and a major phenomenon after that. "We envisioned [metal bats] would open the market to smaller kids. We didn't predict a whole new industry in Tee Ball," Heald tells me.

The low-profile industry that Heald helped to lead in the 1970s has changed. So have the bats that it puts in the hands of children. Today's models are useful in hitting pitched balls. They've also become personal statements and fashion accessories. Like never before, kids' bats feature flashy paint jobs and names seemingly ripped from Terminator movies. Worth's best sellers include Copperhead, Titan, and Toxic, the last of which resembles an orange creamsicle branded with a giant X. Prices exceed that of ice cream on a stick. Worth's 2012 Lithium Prodigy—featuring "Whiplash frame. 30 percent thinner alloy for increased bat speed. Center load end plug for increased inertia"—sells for $199. It's a bargain compared to the Anderson Bat Company's NanoTek XP model; it retails for $300. For off-the-rack sports equipment meant for a twelve-year-old, that's startling.

The bat-sharing and bat-buying paradigm has shifted in youth sports. Players no longer share two or three modestly priced models purchased by the rec league. Now, on a team of twelve or thirteen youth players, most own a personal bat transported in a personal bat bag like a guitar case or attaché. They're like commuters riding the Long Island Railroad.

Who knows whether kid players today are better off than they were twenty years ago, whether they're hitting baseballs farther or having more fun? Certainly pricey sports equipment has exposed economic fault lines among teams and sometimes among teammates. The meritocracy that youth sports used to be is disappearing, and the manufacturers of expensive stuff are playing their part.

Matthew Halsey, a dad from Concord, California, wrote to tell me about an experience he had a summer earlier. His son's 10-and-under traveling team was matched against a team "from a very well-to-do city in Marin County. Every kid on that team had his own composite bat which cost in excess of $200. Not one kid on our team had a new bat, and most were originally purchased for under $150. That said, we played eight innings (two extra) against these kids before finally losing. Proof that having a $250 bat doesn't make you a great hitter."

Halsey added this postscript: "I bought my son's bat at Play It Again Sports for $39."

When I asked Jess Heald whether he'd foreseen the day when a kids' metal bat would cost more than a night at the best hotel in town, all he could do was laugh. "Are you kidding?" he said. Heald's life in youth sports had produced some very positive results for the kids who are today's parents and even grandparents. He wasn't responsible for what came after that.

• • •

Laurie Cronenbold probably would cringe at being described as a youth-sports entrepreneur, though that's exactly what she is. Her venture into the business world hardly defines her, though. Cronenbold lives in Newbury Park, California, near Sherman Oaks. Her husband works for the Los Angeles Fire Department. She has three sons, all capable athletes, and she was a fixture in the stands when they played Little League. One of her recent jobs was driving a fork lift in a warehouse. She is a competent seamstress. She loves horses.

There's another footnote to her bio. Cronenbold is the inventor of the world's first snap-on (and off) athletic supporter—at least the first snap-off jock to have been blessed by the U.S. Patent Office. Cronenbold may make a fortune off of her invention. The thought was not in her mind when she hatched her idea more than a decade ago, however. Her goal was simply to make kids' sports better. It was years before it dawned on her that the supporters she was making for her children and at the request of friends could even become a business. She had simply been following her instincts and trying to help.

In my reporting, I met a number of people with variations on this story. They were busy with their lives. Earning a living in some fashion related to youth sports had hardly entered their minds. Then the unexpected happened: they ended up squarely at the center of the youth sports economy.

That's fortunate for Cronenbold and possibly for male athletes for generations to come. This book isn't intended as a blanket condemnation of youth-sports enterprise.

To the contrary. Some entrepreneurs improve sports for kids—and for their parents too.

Cronenbold is a classic example. She doesn't have a PR firm, and when I found her, she was hardly raking in millions. I was casting a wide net for entrepreneurs with out-of-the box ideas for this book. Among the places I searched was the U.S. Patent office website. Many wild ideas arrive there every day. I typed a few relevant words into the site's search engine and quickly had a list of youth sports innovation. Among them were these: U.S. Pat. No. 6,578,214, a startling line of sports beds featuring football and baseball motifs (the football bed resembles a giant pigskin, down to the radial stripes); U.S. Pat. No. 212,202, a wireless voice transmitter that allows coaches to surreptitiously bark instructions to their players during games; and U.S. Pat. No. 5,535,454, a baseball batting helmet with a cutout just right for girls' ponytails. In this lineup, a snap-off jock seemed entirely reasonable.

Cronenbold's patent application was granted in 2007. When we spoke, three years later, she still was waiting for her product to hit stores' shelves. But that seemed just a matter of time. Cronenbold was different from most entrepreneurs I had spoken with. Mostly she seemed out to prove herself to her children, her neighbors, and to Corporate America.

"I'm not a businessperson," Cronenbold tells me. "I'm a mom. Moms solve problems. I just took this solution a little further than most."

The idea for her product had come slowly, over many months. And it came from her boys. When Tanner, Cronenbold's oldest son, was in the youth league, he'd complain after games about his athletic supporter. As a matter of safety, the undergarment was required for all players in the league. But it was a pain to wear—literally. The hard plastic cup never quite felt comfortable against his skin, a common complaint among kid players.

Laurie decided to do something about her son's problem—or try to—by designing a superior athletic supporter. Her motive was to ease her son's discomfort. There was no business plan. The idea that she might someday be an athletic-supporter mogul would have made her laugh.

An analytical side of Cronenbold began to emerge. She launched an investigation into the ergonomics of the jock. How did it fit, or not fit? How did the cup rest against the skin? What about the shape of the cup? Could the edges be smoothed? She began collecting athletic supporters, shopping local stores, and ordering what she could find on the Web. Her son wore a simple, classic model that rated low on comfort. She wondered about other jock straps, other options.

Cronenbold found all manufacturers essentially made the same product—a triangle of hard plastic dropped into a cloth pouch, which pressed against the most sensitive area of a youth player's anatomy. Boys and men had been playing sports for generations. They'd been wearing—and complaining about—jocks almost as long. Yet nothing better had come along.

In fact, the evolution of the jockstrap is notable for a lack of, well, evolution. The first models appeared in the in the mid-nineteenth century. They were homemade and generally ill-fitting. A supporter that was still on a player's waist at the end of a game was considered a good fit. In the 1920s, a stocking company from Philadelphia, the Guelph Elastic Hosiery Company, got into the jockstrap business, and many competitors followed. There were small innovations after that, of course. But waists and posteriors do not change. By and large, neither had the jockstrap.

In some ways, Cronenbold was as well prepared as anyone could be for the task of rethinking the athletic supporter. In other ways, she admits, she was lost. She collected dozens of jockstraps in her home in Newbury Park. She'd lay them all out on a table, cut the seams with her sewing shears and analyze the pieces. After studying the snaps and elastic bands, she'd sew them back together, substituting new pieces and trying new ideas. If one of her designs looked like it might be an improvement, she'd hand it to her son Tanner, her test pilot. He'd wear the prototype waistband or modified cup to a game. At home that night she'd debrief him, so to speak.

After months of experimentation Cronenbold was making her own supporters from supplies she picked up cheaply—JC Penney boys' briefs, upholstery thread, boating snaps, and "itty bitty Gold Toe socks," which she raided from her boys' bureaus. Each day, she'd record her progress in a notebook, not sure where she was headed but wondering whether it might be by way of the U.S. Patent Office.

Her biggest idea was the snap-on-and-off cup. On February 20, 2007, she became the owner of patent number 7,178,176, "Male Sports/Athletic Protective Undergarment/ Cup System." The eight-page filing is loaded with impressive diagrams—curvy lines tipped with arrows connecting protective cups, shorts, and snaps. On page one, Cronenbold's invention is explained in a one-paragraph abstract:

> An improved male sports/athletic undergarment/cup protective system provides maximum comfort, avoiding stress on the protected body parts while holding the cup securely in its optimal location in the undergarment. A conventional rigid cup is totally covered with a conformal sheath of soft fabric material and fitted externally with a triangular pattern of three snap fastener members made and arranged to removably engage three complementary snap fastener members attached in a matching triangular pattern inside the front panel of a sports/athletic undergarment.

After eleven years of experimentation, Cronenbold had a patent, and perhaps a business. She tells me that companies were intrigued by her idea. Even before her patent was approved, several approached her about buying it, she says. That sounded like a happy story to me. Cronenbold didn't tell it that way. Instead, she told me about paneled conference rooms, lawyers in expensive suits, low-ball offers, hard-ball tactics, stare-downs, face-offs, and ultimatums. It sounded like a scene from the movie *Wall Street*. I had to keep reminding myself that we were talking about jockstraps.

As Cronenbold tells it, one company executive sized up this mother from Newbury Park, California, leaned across a table, and, in a patronizing tone, asked what it would take to buy her patent. She disliked his attitude. "I've been working on this for five years," she recalls saying. "Multiply [your salary] by five, and I'll think about it." Another company insisted she send a prototype jock overnight to Chicago before negotiations opened. She refused. "I wasn't going to let them rip it apart and figure it out," she says.

Cronenbold's situation was not unusual. Business start-ups are vulnerable to being run off the road by established competitors. Nor is it unusual for those companies to buy an innovative idea to protect its share of the market. Cronenbold's response was different. She wasn't interested.

She told me a memorable story that underlined her suspicion of competitors. In the summer of 2004, her athletic supporter reached Williamsport, Pennsylvania, site of the Little League World Series. Cronenbold's middle son, Hayden, and his teammates from the Conejo Valley East Little League in Thousand Oaks beat the long odds, swept through preliminary tournaments in California and the West, and advanced to the annual youth baseball championship for eleven- and twelve-year-olds—a million-to-one shot. Hayden wore the athletic supporter invented by his mom.

So did several of his teammates. During the World Series, the Conejo Valley team lived in dorms on the Little League Baseball campus, where they were fed and their clothes were laundered for them. That meant Hayden's snap-off cup would end up in some communal laundry pile where it might be pilfered by the athletic-supporter competition. That wasn't going to happen, Laurie decided. After games, Laurie and her son met as Hayden left the field. "I'd get the old one," she tells me, "and I'd hand him a new one."

The Conejo Valley East Little League did not win the World Series (Little Leaguers from Willemstad, Curacao, did). Arguably, the bigger story was one that nobody in Williamsport knew that week—the World Series debut of the snap-on supporter.

It took years more to bring the jock to store shelves. Still, Cronenbold's perseverance finally paid off. In 2011 her product was scheduled to make its debut as "Cup Check." The name was her husband's idea. After all, it's a family business.

EIGHT
Beyond Commercialization

Monete Johnson's memory of the day is a bit cloudy. Then again, it was eleven years ago. Here's what she recalls vividly: A surprise assembly in the gym. Bleachers filled with curious, restless kids. A coach moving to the front of the room. A presentation lasting forty-five minutes about a sport "no one in the auditorium had ever heard of—I mean no one," Johnson says.

That sport was squash, hardly a classic urban game. On the streets of inner-city Boston, where Johnson lived, squash just didn't enter the conversation. Yet this day, the coach extended an invitation to those in the room: join a special program that combined instruction in the sport with academic help, mentoring, and community-service opportunities. He called it SquashBusters.

Johnson decided to join. Years later, she says it was one of the wisest decisions of her life—she was now a recent graduate of Trinity College and was looking ahead to earning an advanced degree, perhaps a doctorate in urban policy.

I ask Johnson whether her academic success would have been possible without Squashbusters. Without squash, yes, she says. Without the mentoring she received at Squash-Busters, probably not.

"Growing up, there were few times I could say, 'Hey, I'm proud of myself.' SquashBusters gave me that opportunity," she tells me. "I understood what it's like to make strides, to feel good about yourself."

Monete Johnson is an outgoing, ambitious young woman. And she's a wicked squash player. There's no doubt—this is a story headed for a happy ending. Yet step back and there's a slightly more sobering message to consider: What if there hadn't been a SquashBusters? If Johnson had been sick that day at school? Would she have had a chance in sports?

For kids who live in suburbia there's usually a second chance. There's always a team to join and a sport in season. It works differently in neighborhoods where money doesn't flow easily, neighborhoods without properly maintained fields, where parents work two and three jobs to give their families the basics. For them, organized sports is what other kids do. The idea of playing soccer in a league with coaches, uniforms, goal posts and an inflated ball is a nice dream. But it's a dream.

Thirty years ago, government funding for youth sports largely evaporated. The Reagan Revolution, inspired by President Ronald Reagan, resulted in a dramatic pullback of public support for many community-based programs. Resources for everything from rec centers to salaries for sports counselors were pinched.

As a consequence, millions of kids have been squeezed out of organized sports, including many in urban centers.

These days, kids playing sports—41 million strong— look not to government to pay the bills but to their parents. Jay Coakley, the sport sociologist, has been writing for decades about the "privatization" of youth sports. He points out that this trend has turned youth sports into the private domain of those who can afford it.

In this chapter, the focus is on kids who live in the shadow of commercialization, yet apart from commercialization itself. On the blocks where they live, opportunities to play organized sports are few.

In some neighborhoods, weedy rec fields and underfunded rec centers are discouraging factors. In communities where immigrants live, language is a hurdle. Parents might seek out sports for their children if they knew how.

David Joseph, executive director of America SCORES LA, a nonprofit soccer program in Los Angeles, has seen such problems up close. His soccer program operates in a heavily Latino neighborhood in the heart of Los Angeles. Spanish is the language of the families his program serves. Joseph tells me about the isolation that sometimes results from the language barrier. He recalls a staff member speaking with the father of a teenaged boy who was seeking information about the University of California-Los Angeles. He was eager for his son to apply. Yet most things about the college-application process were a mystery, including the fact that the UCLA campus was five miles away from his home.

How much exposure do inner-city kids get to organized sports compared to kids in the suburbs? What do kids lose when they are excluded by accident of birth—by where they live and what their parents earn—from sports participation?

Up2Us, a New York–based nonprofit that advocates for at-risk kids, has compiled statistics on just this issue. In part, this data reveal that middle-class white kids are far more likely to be sports players than low-income children of color—50 percent more likely.

Girls of color are especially inactive. A study by the University of Pittsburgh tracked the exercise patterns of 1,213 African American girls and 1,166 white girls from ages eight or nine to ages eighteen or nineteen. By the time the girls reached ages sixteen and seventeen, many had pretty much abandoned sports, and 56 percent of African American girls reported no exercise. *None.* For white girls, the figure was 31 percent, also distressingly high.

This generational shift, which is especially acute among the urban poor, is having distressing effects. For one, our kids are getting bigger. By third grade, one in three children in this country is overweight or obese. The problem poses a looming threat to public health and has prompted Michele Obama's "Let's Move" campaign.

Kids who don't exercise pick up other bad habits, according to research. They're more likely to smoke cigarettes and marijuana, and to become abusers of alcohol and illegal drugs. Most disturbing, the number of inactive kids rises every year. According to the Sporting Goods Manufacturers Association, in 2011, 4.5 million kids ages six to twelve didn't exercise at all.

Michelle Obama's efforts are reason to hope for a reversal of this trend sometime soon. Similarly, the work of an array of foundations, philanthropists, and devoted kids' sports advocates is helping a generation of children discover an active lifestyle.

Ed Snider bought the expansion Philadelphia Flyers of the National Hockey League in 1967. Seven years later, his Broad Street Bullies, named for their physical play, became the first NHL expansion franchise in history to win the coveted Stanley Cup as league champions. Snider's devotion to hockey and to Philadelphia has since morphed in a wonderful new way.

In 2005, he launched a youth-hockey foundation that brings the sport to city kids. Recently, the foundation donated $5.5 million to renovate three city rinks and fund skating lessons, leagues, and after-school programs. "I do want this to be my legacy," Snider, nearing eighty, said. "I want to fund it in such a way—and establish it in such a way—that it's something that will last forever."

In 1999, the Walter and Evelyn Haas Foundation created Team-Up for Youth, a kids' program designed to bring sports back to resource-strapped schools in the San Francisco Bay area. The Haas clan already was in the habit of taking on big sports challenges. The prominent San Franciscans are the founding family of Levi Strauss, which quite possibly made the jeans you are wearing now. From 1980 to 1995, they also owned the Oakland Athletics of Major League Baseball, heady years in which the team contended often and won a World Series title, in 1989.

Walter Haas Jr. tells me that the family's experience owning the baseball team greatly affected its decision to launch a nonprofit aimed at kids and sports. Wally, as he's known, says that, as a team owner, "you see firsthand the power of sports to captivate kids in a deep and meaning-ful way—unlike anything else I've experienced. It gave me the idea, What if we could use sports as a hook to give certain kids who didn't have much opportunity the things they need?"

In the years since, the Haas Foundation has backed Team-Up for Youth with gifts of nearly $11 million, doing good in communities that badly need help. One initiative, Coaching Corps, has trained and placed more than 1,500 volunteer coaches in youth programs—significantly, 60 per-cent of these coaches are women.

Around the country, dozens of other programs are reach-ing kids in need. One of the most inspiring is SquashBusters. Its founder, Greg Zaff, is a true hero of youth sports. Few people could have envisioned an organization like Squash-Busters, much less started one. It required someone steeped in the sport of squash, with business know-how and, most important, who was moved by the plight of city kids.

Zaff played squash at Williams College and then took his racket to the professional ranks for seven years. Later, as a student at Harvard's Kennedy School of Government, he wrote a paper about an urban squash program—one that did not yet exist—that would reach out to disadvantaged kids. His belief was that the sport could engage kids physically, as well as put them on the road to successful lives.

SquashBusters is not all about squash, and it's definitely not for children seeking the path of least resistance. Kids enter the program as sixth graders. But only a fraction of those who apply are accepted. Program leaders carefully review many students before narrowing consideration to those who are "the best students, the hardest workers, the most dedicated kids who want it the most," Zaff says.

Next, SquashBusters' counselors meet with parents to gauge their commitment to the program and its goals. The relatively few children in the running at that stage are invited to sign a "participation agreement" officially admitting them to the wonderful club.

Squash has lifted the futures of more than a thousand kids in Boston alone since Zaff launched the program. These days, there are 100 to 130 kids involved each year in Boston. In other cities, Zaff is busy replicating SquashBusters' success. With several fellow urban-squash activists, he founded the National Urban Squash and Education Association, of which he is executive director. Through its efforts, kids are playing the sport in Baltimore, the Bronx, Chicago, Denver, New Haven, Philadelphia, and San Diego.

Zaff and his colleagues are adamant that these programs teach more than squash. In Boston, kids agree to spend nine hours a week with their SquashBusters friends and mentors—three days a week for three hours at a stretch. Practices and matches are held at a state-of-the-art squash center that SquashBusters built on the campus of Northeastern University with money from private donors. The center includes eight courts and, notably, three classrooms, where the talk is of high school courses and ambition to attend college.

Big dreams take shape. In SquashBusters' short existence, 100 percent of participants have graduated high school (compared to 70 percent overall in the Boston's public high schools). And 85 percent have continued their education at four-year colleges such as Cornell, Brown, and, in Monete Johnson's case, Trinity. That is nearly twice the rate for the overall student population in Boston's city high schools.

Zaff points out that for this life-altering experience the SquashBusters' kids pay virtually nothing. The program absorbs the costs of instruction, court time, travel, classroom mentoring, and college guidance. There's even a clothing allowance for squash uniforms, though Zaff explains, "We do ask them to put a little money into that."

I ask Monete Johnson what kids take away from Squash-Busters other than those sharp uniforms.

"Kids need a sense of accomplishment. Not to win all the time, but to work hard at something that belongs to them," she tells me. It is a message she may be sharing with the next class of SquashBusters' recruits. A few months after we spoke, she hoped to begin her first post-college job—as a SquashBusters counselor.

America SCORES doesn't rescue kids with a squash ball. In some ways, it's quite different from Greg Zaff's program. It's located in the center of Los Angeles, hooks kids with a sport

they are familiar with, and makes the most of subpar facilities. The organization holds many practices and games not
on manicured fields or even grass fields.

Still, in ways that matter most, SquashBusters and America SCORES are similar. Both reach into neighborhoods in
which sports commercialization is absent, because, for the
most part, sports for kids is missing too. America SCORES
began in 1994 in the classroom of a Washington, DC, public
school teacher, Julie Kennedy. To keep her students occupied and out of trouble, Kennedy launched a soccer program
for girls. When foul weather forced her girls inside, Kennedy
did what coaches often do (not really)—she introduced them
to poetry. The unlikely combination fit together surprisingly
well, engaging mind and body in ways that kids responded
to. (The same was true when Kennedy later added a third
component, community service.) Today, America SCORES
operates in fifteen cities where it inspires more than 4,500
"poet-athletes."

David Joseph, the executive director of America SCORES
in Los Angeles, filled me in on how the program operates.
When America SCORES arrived in LA, it consulted the public school system about choosing a neighborhood in which it
could do the most good. Fingers pointed to the Palms community on the city's West Side. Like many places in LA, the
neighborhood is low income and densely populated with
non-English-speaking immigrants. Nearly thirty thousand
people, almost all renters, pack the tiny street grid. What
captured the attention of America SCORES, though, is
what is missing from the Palms neighborhood. It lacks a
library, a nearby park, a YMCA rec center, a blade of grass.

Safe recreation was greatly needed here, Joseph tells
me. So was hope. The obstacles that face kids every day are
daunting—poverty, isolation, and the overwhelming sense

that there is no way out. Organized youth sports also were missing. Most kids enrolled in America SCORES have had minimal experience playing in sports leagues. "When we get them in the third grade," Joseph says, "the majority have no experience."

These days, America SCORES operates in four elementary and middle schools in the Palms community. Counting alumni who remain involved, four hundred children are in the program's orbit.

Some terrific soccer players have emerged from America SCORES. They play on their high school teams and sometimes into college. But the real goal is to wake up kids to the talents they have and that often go unrecognized.

Joseph tells me the story of a young girl whose journey seems to illustrate all the good things that America SCORES and other sports-outreach efforts offer. Mireya Mateo entered America SCORES as a fourth grader at Palms Elementary School, having never played a minute of organized soccer.

She took to the game quickly and, just as fast, became an accomplished poet, in keeping with the literary emphasis of America SCORES. That progress continued year after year until Mateo reached Alexander Hamilton High School in LA. By then, she had become one of the most complete student-athletes that the program had ever developed. Her grade point average hovered at around 3.6 (out of a possible 4.0). And her sports credentials were impressive: Mateo ran varsity cross-country, completed four Los Angeles Marathons, and, yes, was captain of her high school soccer team. In the fall of 2011, she was headed to college at the University of California-Santa Cruz.

David Joseph shared a poem that Mateo penned when she entered the program, a poem about discovering soccer through America SCORES. It was an eleven-year-old's first crack at creative writing and a major success, winning first prize—and a free trip to a World Cup soccer game—in a contest sponsored by Yahoo. "Soccer is Family" ended with these verses:

> Being on a soccer team
> is like being in a family.
> On a team, you help each other
> and you cheer for each other.
> My team is The Killer Whales.
> My team is a family too.

Not all programs that serve needy kids serve only them. Some cross economic and neighborhood lines to be social levelers. Kids become teammates and friends learning that those differences aren't important. In that category are two all-star organizations: Girls on the Run and Row New York.

I'm a weekend runner, so for me there's a lot to admire about Girls on the Run. Turning adolescent girls into elite marathoners isn't the goal of this national program. Rather, its focus is helping young women test their limits and expand them. Girls meet twice a week for training over a twelve-week session. As a final test, they're challenged by a 3.1-mile "running event." Some are hooked on running by then. At least all have had three months of exercise and sessions with mentors, and all have wrestled with such tough developmental issues as "standing up to peer pressure," "gossiping hurts everyone," and "it's okay to choose my friends."

Girls on the Run also underscores a reality about youth sports—rarely are programs able to escape the clutches of corporate sponsorship. This nonprofit receives support from foundations and generous individuals. It also cashes checks from New Balance, Kellogg's Frosted Flakes, and Secret deodorant. (Maybe Fuse marketing guru Bill Carter was right—corporate dollars have a [limited] place in youth sports.)

Row New York girls' program is another that deserves mention. Since 2002, girls across New York City have been showing up at a boathouse in Queens to push themselves in ways they hadn't imagined. Its purpose is two-fold— assembling a darn good rowing team and, at the same time, "empowering young people to pursue excellence in all facets of their lives."

Row New York isn't for couch potatoes. Girls in the "competitive" program are on the water five days a week— Tuesdays through Fridays after school and Saturday mornings from nine to noon. On Mondays, Row New York girls receive academic assistance. The long stretches of time spent together—and the intensity of those experiences— often create strong bonds. It doesn't matter whether the girls live on Central Park or in a tenement apartment. They're all pulling in the same direction.

I was impressed with what I'd heard and read about programs like SquashBusters and Girls on the Run. They seem to strike a careful balance between sport for fun and sport for a greater purpose. I wasn't certain what I was responding to. Was it that many of these kids would have been left out of organized sports if not for the nonprofits bringing recreation and hope to their neighborhoods? That these programs sometimes are melting pots, hangouts where kids from differing cultures rally behind a common goal?

No doubt, it is a starkly different experience than ones found on many sports teams in suburbia. Certainly, there is less emphasis on having the latest soccer cleats and traveling to the most elite tournaments.

For me, it raises the question: Which are the privileged kids?

I asked Greg Zaff of SquashBusters whether the students in his inner-city programs considered themselves to be low income or disadvantaged. Other might use such labels to describe their lives. But would they? He thought for a few seconds. "In squash you see phenomenal affluence," Zaff says. "It's not unheard of for a parent to hire a coach for $50,000 a year basically to come to their house to work with a child or to take them to a private court, basically to be at their beck and call. Then you have people"—he paused again—"who don't have a lot.

"I don't think kids spend a lot of time feeling sorry for themselves. There isn't a lot of 'Woe is me, isn't my life terrible. I'm this poor little kid,'" Zaff continues. "For one thing, they're not all poor. Some are. But the stereotype that all the kids in our program live in abject poverty isn't true."

David Joseph of America SCORES echoes that. Even kids living on a knife's edge rarely speak of being poor, he tells me. In fact, the opposite is true. When America SCORES goes into the community to do good-works projects, the kids in his program pointedly talk about helping poor people. "They don't see themselves as being at risk, as victims," Joseph says. "That's a good thing."

Maybe living outside the mainstream of sports commercialization isn't entirely a bad thing. Maybe it's to be envied.

"In some ways watching them has me rethinking my own athletic experience," Joseph says. "To see how much joy they play with, whether they're playing on a field or an alley. It's kind of a pure experience, like one endless pickup game."

POSTSCRIPT

Heading into any nonfiction book project, an author wonders: Where will my material come from? Well, almost any book project. I was fortunate that rarely a week went by in which a friend, colleague, or blood relative did not contact me with a note beginning, "Have you heard about this???!!!"

Though I'd been working on this book more than a year, often I hadn't heard of these tips and ideas. Some made their way into the book. Many did not. (Sorry about the omission of EyeBlack.com, the key to controlling youth sports glare "without the greasy mess.") A good number of these leads underscored the central message of the book, or the one I intended: that some companies and shrewd individuals have colonized youth sports in ways that have made them much more stressful and expensive, turning parents and even kids into consumers of products they had no idea they needed— or even wanted. In the end, what's for sale usually isn't eye black or any such thing. Instead, it's hope—hope that investing a hundred or a thousand dollars may advance a child's sports career just a little bit. And if it doesn't? Well, we've fulfilled our obligations as dutiful parents and given our kids every conceivable edge.

For me, this book meant more than just wrestling with these ideas. Perhaps the most pleasurable part of the project was my role as an accidental tourist, meeting with and listening to dozens of people connected in some fashion to the youth sports economy. With each conversation, I learned more about what I didn't know. That kept me pressing ahead, out of curiosity and sometimes fear.

I was lucky to cross paths with Fran Dicari, the Cincinnati dad and sports parenting blogger. Fran follows the money like no one else I met on this project. He also appreciates the value of supporting his kids in sports. Check out his blog—and tell him I sent you—at StatsDad.com. I thank the U.S. Patent Office website for leading me to Laurie Cronenbold, who launched her sports business because her boys needed, ahem, special support. Bill Carter, the head of Fuse Marketing, contributed a key perspective, keeping me alert to the balance between what Corporate America takes from youth sports and what it gives. Finally, I tip my cap to sports sociologist Jay Coakley. If I'm ever asked to appoint a youth sports czar in America, Jay is on my short list.

ACKNOWLEDGMENTS

I'm responsible for the reporting in this book. The ideas—including the muddled ones—are mine, too. Still, many people contributed to the project in important ways.

I wish to thank Andrew Blauner, my literary agent, for making the right call once again. At Beacon Press, I am grateful to my editor, Helene Atwan, who proposed the idea for this project and improved the manuscript with each read. Susan Lumenello, Jessie Bennett, and Allison Trzop also pitched in at critical times.

Thanks to the many who pushed the project forward in more ways than I can count. They include Jesse Yomtov, Ron Stein, Dirk Buikema, Jim Dale, Richard Vatz, Michael Bryant, Mike Ricigliano, Jack Gibbons, Ken Rosenthal, Brad Snyder, Josh Barr, George Solomon, Alan Schwarz, Tom Farrey, Joe Jacobs, Lisa Delpy Neirotti, Sandy Banisky, Michael Ollove, Rob Slade, Deb Jacobson, Elizabeth Rice, Mary Page Michel, Jerome and Helen Jones, Kenn and Marcia Finkel, Kelsey Twist Schroeder, Anne Chorske Stuzin, Kim Simons, Paul Bernstorf, John Timson, Maya Hyman, Lia Hyman, and Mima Jimenez-Hyman.

Thanks to Jim Thompson and David Jacobson at the Positive Coaching Alliance, Nancy Yawn at the Round Rock Convention and Visitors Bureau, Megan Bartlett at Up2Us, and Janet Carter at Team-Up for Youth. I received important research assistance from Jon Kendle of the Pro Football

Hall of Fame, Marguerite Moran at the Ford Motor Company Archives, and Venus Van Ness at the Norman Rockwell Museum.

Finally, I'm grateful for the support of my wife, Peggy, and our sons, Eli and Ben. Thanks for everything, before, and after, deadline.

WORKS CITED

Author interviews were conducted on the phone, via e-mail, and in person between January 2000 and May 2011.

Introduction

Author interviews with Greg Centracchio, Frank Smoll, Jay Coakley, and Michael Messner.

Mark Hyman, "Can't Make Your Child's Game? Break Out the Laptop," *New York Times,* August 25, 2010.

"Family Life: Where We Stand: TV Viewing Time," Healthy Children.org, May 19, 2011.

Chapter One: The Parent Trap

Author interviews with Roc Murray, Fran Dicari, Cheri McKinney, Dennis Anderson, and Luis Pico.

Mark Hyman, "Reading, Writing—and Winning: With Its Star Trainers and Demanding Regimen, IMG Academies Is More Than a Sports Camp—and Far Pricier," *BusinessWeek,* April 2, 2001.

Jake Nordbye, "Update: Ellsworth Airman's Family Stung by Anderson at the Sum of $6,300," Inside Dakota Sports, July 13, 2010.

StatsDad, "Youth Volleyball," StatsDad.com, January 9, 2011.

Chapter Two: Baby Goes Pro

Author interviews with Doreen Bolhuis, Matt Hendison, Bob Bingham, Don Crowe, Gigi Fernandez, Bob Bigelow, Lyle Micheli, and Lisa Mullen.

Susan Gregory Thomas, *Buy, Buy Baby: How Consumer Culture*

Manipulates Parents and Harms Young Minds (Boston: Houghton Mifflin Harcourt, 2007).

Mark Hyman, "For the Goal-Oriented Parent, a Jump Start in Toddler Sports," *New York Times,* December 6, 2010 (orig. "Sports Training Has Begun for Babies and Toddlers," November 30, 2010).

Tamar Lewin, "No Einstein in Your Crib? Get a Refund," *New York Times,* October 23, 2009.

Chapter Three: Youth Sports, USA

Author interviews with Sharon Prete, Marilyn Porter, Mike Robinson, Dan Vaughn, Juan Garcia, Andrew Zimbalist, Don Schumacher, and Nancy Yawn. I also benefitted from information provided by Matthew Klein, manager, capital budget, Maryland General Assembly.

Sam Boykin, "Wishful Pitch: Mooresville, Iredell County Banking on Youth Baseball Bonanza," *Mecklenburg (NC) Times,* May 18, 2010.

Ryan Sharrow, "Debt-Laden Aberdeen Seeks Hotel Tax to Pay for Ripken Stadium," *Baltimore Business Journal,* September 28, 2009.

Doug Smith, "Disney Builds Magical Facilities for Athletes of All Ages," *USA Today,* September 9, 2008.

Katie Thomas, "Girls' Sports Pack Economic Punch," *New York Times,* July 28, 2009.

Tribune Staff, "CVB Events to Salute Travel," *South Bend (IN) Tribune,* May 7, 2010.

Chapter Four: The Sponsorship Game

Author interviews with Bill Carter, Jay Coakley, David Hyman, and Lee Iacocca.

American Academy of Pediatrics, "Kids Should Not Consume Energy Drinks, and Rarely Need Sports Drinks," news release, May 30, 2001.

Dave Brady, "Wilkinson Tells Writers: If Fitness Is a Joke, This Country Has Had It," *Washington Post Times-Herald,* August 5, 1961 (PP&K quote).

"The Effect of Soda on Teeth," *Good Morning America*, ABC-TV, February 13, 2009.

Gerald Eskenazi, "N.H.L. Looks to Skate, Shoot and Score," *New York Times*, August 30, 1970.

Tom Farrey, "A Legal Performance-Enhancing Drink: Caffeine-Loaded Energy Drinks, Popular with High School Athletes, Largely Unregulated," *E:60*, ESPN.com, October 27, 2010.

Todd Jones et al., "Children May Be Vulnerable in $5 Billion Youth-Sports Industry," *Columbus Dispatch*, August 27, 2010.

Tripp Mickle and Terry Lefton, "Will Action Star White Take Flight from Red Bull?" *Sports Business Journal*, June 6, 2011.

William Neuman, "Save the Children Breaks With Soda Tax Effort," *New York Times*, December 14, 2010.

Bill Pennington, "Reading, Writing and Corporate Sponsorships," *New York Times*, October 18, 2004.

"'61 Home Runs!" *New York Times*, September 20, 1961 (PP&K ad).

Sports Business Journal, "Top 25 Sports Spenders, Their Ad Spending, Key Executives, Agencies and Sponsorships," May 10, 2010.

Dan Wetzel, "Let Them Pay," *Yahoo! Sports*, August 23, 2006.

Chapter Five: Exposed and Overexposed

Author interviews with Tony Martin, Stu Vetter, Dan McMahon, Buzz Bissinger, Jim Taylor, Rashid Ghazi, and Monte Lorell.

Jenny Dial, "Basketball Team's 170 Points Produces Record, Controversy," *Houston Chronicle*, January 6, 2010.

Eli Saslow, "Vetter, the Innovator, Is Still Showing 'Em," *Washington Post*, December 24, 2006.

Jim Taylor, *Positive Pushing: How to Raise a Successful and Happy Child* (New York: Hyperion, 2002).

Phil Taylor, "March Madness Comes to High School Hoops," *Sports Illustrated*, April 13, 2009.

Gene Wojciechowski, "College 'Recruit's' Lie a Tale Gone Horribly Wrong," ESPN.com, February 8, 2008.

Chapter Six: Selling Hope

Author interviews with Patrick Marsh; Andy Bark; Vern Gambetta; J. C. Pinkney; father of Abby (name withheld), athlete listed at beRecruited; Mike Zandler; Tara Vanderveer; and Ricky Fried. Interviews at the Baltimore SPARQ event conducted by journalists Jesse Yomtov and Ron Stein, who provided audiotapes to me; interview subjects: Christopher Shaw, Lucas Smissen, Randall Anderson, Ebenezer Ogundeko, Eamon Van-Callahan, and Dustin Baker.

Matthew Futterman, "The Do-It-Yourself Athletic Scholarship," *Wall Street Journal*, December 18, 2008.

Tripp Mickle, "UA Partners with Scout.com to Host Football Combines," *Sports Business Journal*, May 5, 2008.

"Scholarships: Slicing the Pie," graphic, *New York Times*, March 10, 2008.

Schuman's National Underclassmen Combine, "Largest National High School Football Combine Camp Announces Expansion and 2011 Combine Schedule," news release, August 18, 2010.

Jason P. Skoda, "High School Combines Range in Price, Legitimacy Making It Vital to Choose Right One," *East Valley (AZ) Tribune*, March 27, 2011.

Chapter Seven: Making Progress, and Maybe a Fortune

Author interviews with Brendan Sullivan, Jess Heald, and Laurie Cronenbold.

Chapter Eight: Beyond Commercialization

Author interviews with Monete Johnson, Jay Coakley, Walter Haas Jr., Greg Zaff, and David Joseph.

P. W. Baumert et al., "Health Risk Behaviors of Adolescent Participants in Organized Sports," *Journal of Adolescent Health* 22 (1998): 460–65 (cigarettes/marijuana study).

Sue Y. S. Kimm et al., "Decline in Physical Activity in Black Girls and White Girls during Adolescence," *New England Journal of Medicine* 347 (September 2002): 709–15 (Pittsburgh study).

J. F. Pirro, "Giving on the Main Line: Main Liners Find Unique Ways to Contribute," *Main Line Today* (PA), November 24, 2009 (Snider quote).

R. Riley et al., *Afterschool Programs: Keeping Children Safe and Smart* (Washington, DC: Child Trends, 2000) (drugs/alcohol study).

INDEX